HISTORY & GEOGRAPHY
The Civil War (1855–1880)

LIFEPAC Test is located at the back of the booklet. Please remove before starting the unit.

Author:
Theresa Buskey, B.A., J.D.

Editor:
Alan Christopherson, M.S.

Westover Studios Design Team:
Phillip Pettet, Creative Lead
Teresa Davis, DTP Lead
Nick Castro
Andi Graham
Jerry Wingo

804 N. 2nd Ave. E.
Rock Rapids, IA 51246-1759

The Civil War (1855–1880)

Introduction

"A house divided against itself cannot stand. I believe this government cannot endure permanently half slave and half free. I do not expect the Union to be dissolved—I do not expect the house to fall—but I do expect it will cease to be divided. It will become all one thing, or all the other." Abraham Lincoln spoke these words in 1858, just two years before the beginning of his presidency and the Civil War. They reflected the storm gathering across the nation that would soon empty its heavy clouds on the heads of the Union in one of America's costliest wars.

The years from 1855 to 1880 were some of the darkest in the history of our nation. In fact, the nation almost ceased to exist during those years. In some cases, the Civil War literally pitted brother against brother. It finally settled the issue of slavery and the permanence of the Union. The years that followed the war were blackened by revenge, greed, and failure to protect the newly freed slaves. The restoration of the Union was as much in question as its survival once was, but again the nation survived. A South without slavery was reintegrated into a stronger United States of America.

This LIFEPAC® will cover the critical years from 1855 to 1880. We will present the increasing hostility and distrust between the North and the South, the events within and those that led to the Civil War, and finally the difficult post-war Reconstruction.

Objectives

Read these objectives. The objectives tell you what you will be able to do when you have successfully completed this LIFEPAC. When you have finished this LIFEPAC, you should be able to:

1. Discuss why and how the North and South split.

2. Name the major events that led up to the Civil War.

3. Describe how secession occurred.

4. List the advantages of both sides in the Civil War.

5. Describe the major battles and the course of the Civil War.

6. Describe Reconstruction.

7. Describe the background and policies of Civil War-era presidents.

8. Describe the post-Civil War corruption.

9. Explain the status of black Americans during and after Reconstruction.

Survey the LIFEPAC. Ask yourself some questions about this study and write your questions here.

1. INCREASING DISUNION

The era of compromise had ended with the Kansas-Nebraska Act in 1854. The Whig Party had fallen apart over disagreements about slavery, and the Democratic Party was soon split over it also. Several denominations, including Baptists, Methodists, and Presbyterians also split between North and South over the controversy. The two sides were becoming more hardened and less willing to discuss their positions. The Union was in grave danger.

The rhetoric of the two sides left less and less room for compromise during the last few years of the 1850s. The publicity of the Lincoln-Douglas debates gave a national following to Abraham Lincoln who steadfastly opposed slavery as immoral. The pro-slavery Dred Scott decision by the Supreme Court was denounced in the North as invalid. A financial crash that did not disturb the South as much as the North was seen in their own eyes as proof of the South's superior position.

A whole series of violent incidents marked the last five years before the Civil War. A small civil war broke out in "Bleeding Kansas" over the issue of whether or not it would be a slave state. On the Senate floor, a Southern congressman beat a Northern senator with a cane. John Brown led a raid into Virginia, intending to start up a slave revolt and instead became an abolitionist martyr. The verbal hostility of previous years became increasingly physical.

The South felt threatened by the growing abolitionist movement and political power of the North. The last straw was the election of a Republican president in 1860. The Republican Party was a Northern, anti-slavery party, and the South would not tolerate such a party to rule over them. Eleven states seceded from the Union. The war began in April of 1861 when the Southern army at Charleston fired on a federal outpost named Fort Sumter in their harbor.

SECTION OBJECTIVES

Review these objectives. When you have completed this section, you should be able to:

1.   Discuss why and how the North and South split.

2.   Name the major events that led up to the Civil War.

3.   Describe how secession occurred.

4.   List the advantages of both sides in the Civil War.

7.   Describe the background and policies of Civil War-era presidents.

VOCABULARY

Study these words to enhance your learning success in this section.

arsenal (är' se nal). A building for the manufacture or storage of arms, ammunition, and military equipment.

disavow (dis a vou'). To deny responsibility.

egalitarian (ē gal i ter' ē an). Marked by a belief in human equality, especially in respect to social, economic, and political rights and privileges.

exacerbate (ig zas' er bāt). To make more violent, bitter, or severe.

AMERICA from 1855 to 1880

Franklin Pierce
1853-1857
Democratic

James Buchanan
1857-1861
Democratic

Abraham Lincoln*
1861-1865
Republican

Andrew Johnson
1865-1869
Republican

Ulysses S. Grant
1869-1877
Republican

Rutherford B. Hayes
1877-1881
Republican

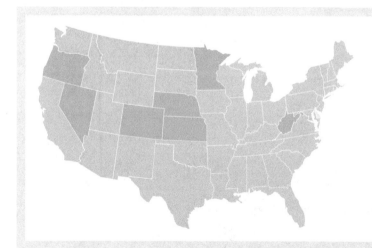

STATES ADMITTED TO THE UNION

Minnesota	1858
Oregon	1859
Kansas	1861
West Virginia	1863
Nevada	1864
Nebraska	1867
Colorado	1876

POPULATION of the United States of America

Year	Population
1880	50,189,209
1850	23,191,876
1820	9,638,453
1790	3,929,000

*assassinated while in office

repercussion (rē per kush' un). A widespread, indirect, or unforeseen effect of an act, action, or event.

segregate (seg' re gāt). To separate people of different races by having separate facilities like schools, restaurants, and theatres for each race.

Note: *All vocabulary words in this LIFEPAC appear in* boldface *print the first time they are used. If you are not sure of the meaning when you are reading, study the definitions given.*

Pronunciation Key: hat, āge, cãre, fär; let, ēqual, tėrm; it, īce; hot, ōpen, ôrder; oil; out; cup, pu̇t, rüle; child; long; thin; /ŦH/ for then; /zh/ for measure; /u/ or /ə/ represents /a/ in about, /e/ in taken, /i/ in pencil, /o/ in lemon, and /u/ in circus.

Division and Violence

The South. The slave states of the South in 1855 had a unique culture; they thought of themselves as virtually a separate nation. They believed they had a better way of life than the North. The South clung to older notions of an "aristocratic" class long after it had been abandoned by the rest of the nation. Its population was stagnant, and few immigrants came to the South because there were few opportunities there. The population was more uniformly people of British background whose families had lived in America for generations. A strict class system existed with wealthy planters at the top and slaves at the bottom. Southerners believed this was an ideal society and looked down on the **egalitarian** North.

The South was agricultural. It had little manufacturing. The factories that did exist were smaller and employed fewer people than those in either the North or northwest. The main cash crop was cotton with tobacco, rice, and sugar cane as alternatives in some areas. These crops were very labor intensive and were raised primarily on large plantations by enslaved people. Only about one-quarter of Southern families owned slaves. Those that did not often practiced subsistence agriculture. Even those without slaves supported the plantation system. Even the poorest white man had status above the enslaved black people.

By 1855, the South was very concerned about the threat from the North to their way of life. The North's growing population had given them complete control of the House of Representatives. The Compromise of 1850 had left the North in control of the Senate. The North had its own political party, the Republicans, which was rapidly gaining popularity and offices. The South equated the Republican Party with the radical abolitionists who spoke of fighting and slave revolts in order to end slavery in the South. The Republican Party pledged not to attack slavery where it existed, but only to prevent its spread. Most Southerners did not trust those statements. The Democratic Party still had supporters in both the North and South. Southerners looked to it as one of the last united institutions in the nation.

Abolitionists. Anti-slavery sentiment had existed in America for many years, but the serious, organized movement that so frightened the South began in the 1830s. In 1831, William Lloyd Garrison began publishing the anti-slavery newspaper, the *Liberator*. In 1833 Parliament voted to end slavery in the British West Indies. That same year, the American Anti-Slavery Society was formed with about sixty members. Within five years, it had grown to about 250,000 people. Hundreds of other societies devoted to the end of human bondage

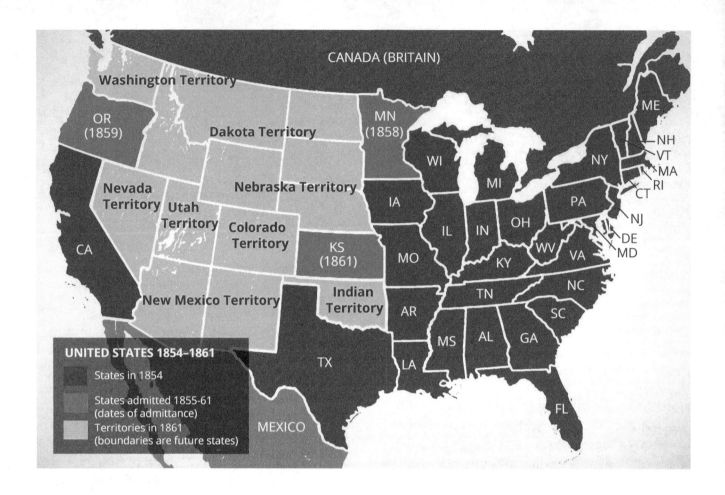

CANADA (BRITAIN)

Washington Territory

OR (1859)

Dakota Territory

MN (1858)

ME

NH
VT
MA
RI
CT

Nevada Territory

Utah Territory

Nebraska Territory

WI

MI

NY

PA

NJ
DE
MD

Colorado Territory

IA

IL IN OH

CA

KS (1861)

MO

KY WV VA

New Mexico Territory

Indian Territory

AR

TN

NC

SC

MS AL GA

TX

LA

FL

UNITED STATES 1854–1861

States in 1854

States admitted 1855-61 (dates of admittance)

Territories in 1861 (boundaries are future states)

MEXICO

were formed all over the North in the late 1830s. Many of these people were Christians putting feet on their faith. These organizations worked by lobbying, organizing rallies, printing literature, publishing stories, and petitioning the government.

However, abolitionists were unpopular radicals for many years. The South and Southern sympathizers reacted to their work with repression and violence. Abolitionist works were banned in the South. People were imprisoned for even possessing them. Mobs attacked prominent abolitionists. Printing presses were destroyed, and anti-slavery speakers were pelted with filth when they spoke. Even Northern politicians tried to distance themselves from the abolitionist views. It had been an unspoken policy of both the Democrats and the Whigs to avoid the issue of slavery entirely, which they did for many years.

Gradually, these determined advocates won their point in the North. The issue of slavery was finally taken out of hiding. The continued discussions forced people to look and see what was happening in their nation. Millions of people were being held in bondage. The Fugitive Slave Act brought the issue home to many in the North. Eventually, when the Whigs and Democrats still avoided the issue, the Republicans took it up to squarely and rapidly become a powerful force in the North.

Bleeding Kansas. After the Kansas-Nebraska Act of 1854, Kansas was to choose for itself on the issue of slavery. It was west of the slave state of Missouri, and many Southerners expected to make it a slave state as well. Most of the settlers came from the North with its larger population. Some of the Northerners were sponsored by abolitionist societies who wanted to make sure that Kansas had a good supply of anti-slave settlers. Missouri responded by sending its own pro-slave settlers supported by well-armed bands of Missouri citizens. Both sides were hostile and violent in what became known as "Bleeding Kansas."

Conflict in both the political and physical areas ruled in Kansas. When the territory voted for its first legislature in 1855, Missouri pro-slavers crossed the border and voted illegally, giving the pro-slavery people control of the new government. The free-soil supporters formed their own illegal government at Topeka to counter it. A pro-slavery "posse" invaded the anti-slavery town of Lawrence in 1856 to arrest members of the illegal government, looting and burning the town. A violent (and possibly insane) abolitionist named John Brown butchered five pro-slavery men in Pottawatomie Creek in response.

By 1857 Kansas had enough people to apply for statehood. The majority of the population was anti-slavery, but the legislature was under the control of the pro-slavery group. The state had to vote on the issue of slavery to comply with "popular sovereignty," so the legislature created a shifty document known as the Lecompton Constitution. The people were allowed to vote only on the constitution, with or without slavery. But the constitution itself protected slavery. Even if the people voted for it to be free, Kansas would still be a slave state. The free-soil people boycotted the election, and the constitution passed with slavery. It was sent to Washington as the basis for admitting Kansas to the Union.

The Caning of Sumner. Charles Sumner was a radical abolitionist member of the Senate. In May of 1856, he delivered a scathing two-day speech on "The Crime against Kansas." His colorful rhetoric was very insulting to the South. He also made some vulgar insults against South Carolina's Senator Andrew Butler. The speech was not well received by his Northern colleagues. Even William Seward, abolitionist leader of Congress, did not approve of his language.

| Bleeding Kansas

Sumner's speech was considered a personal insult by Congressman Preston Brooks, a relative of Butler's. He decided to deal with the senator personally. Brooks decided against challenging him to a duel, since he believed Sumner to be his social inferior, and it was likely the Northerner would refuse. Instead, he decided to beat him to redress the insult.

On May 22nd, Brooks walked into the Senate chamber and approached Sumner, who was sitting at his desk. He raised his cane and proceeded to beat the helpless man about the head and shoulders until the cane broke. Finally, someone stopped Brooks, and Sumner was carried away unconscious.

What was remarkable about the incident was the difference between the reactions in the North and the South. People in the North saw it as a use of force to stop anti-slavery speech, and it drew a great deal of abolitionist publicity. Sumner was voted back into his seat in the Senate, even though it was three years before he was well enough to serve. In the South, Brooks was hailed as a hero. Hundreds of people sent him new canes to replace the one he had broken. His constituents voted him back into the House of Representatives after he resigned because of the incident. The difference in the reactions highlighted a dangerous separation between the two sides.

Election of 1856. In 1856, the Democrats managed to unite behind one candidate, James Buchanan. Most of the potential candidates for president were tainted by the Kansas-Nebraska Act and could not gain the support of Northern Democrats. Buchanan had been acting as the American minister in Great Britain from 1852-1856 and was therefore "safe" on the issue. Buchanan avoided the topic of slavery as much as possible and argued for the preservation of the Union.

Buchanan was opposed by the Republican candidate John Frémont, called "the Pathfinder" for his work mapping routes and sites for forts in the west. The Republicans campaigned on the issue of no slavery in the territories. "Free soil, free men, and Frémont" was their slogan. Millard Fillmore was a candidate for the Know-Nothing Party and also had the support of the dying Whig Party. The two-year-old Republican Party made a remarkable showing, winning eleven states, all in the North. However, the still barely unified Democrats won the election, putting James Buchanan in the White House.

James Buchanan. James Buchanan (1791-1868) was the only U.S. president never to marry. He entered the White House with impressive credentials. He had been born to immigrant parents in Pennsylvania and became a prosperous lawyer in that state. He began his political career as a Federalist, but eventually became a strong Democrat supporter of Andrew Jackson. He had served in the Pennsylvania legislature and as a soldier in the War of 1812. He had

| James Buchanan, the only U.S. president never to marry

served in both the House and Senate in Washington. He was secretary of state under James Polk and represented America in both Russia and Britain.

Buchanan lacked strong convictions on the issue of slavery and tended to be pro-Southern in his policies. He did not have the fortitude or the foresight to deal with the rising divisions in the nation. When the Lecompton Constitution was presented to Congress, Buchanan backed it without quibbling about its origins. Stephen Douglas showed that he was made of sterner stuff. He had proposed popular sovereignty for the territories, and he meant it to be just that! He successfully opposed the admission of Kansas under the dubious document. Instead, it was sent back for a vote on the whole constitution. The anti-slavery voters in Kansas rejected it. But with the ongoing conflict, it was not until 1861 that the state was finally able to organize a genuine constitution and be admitted to the Union.

✎ **Complete these sentences.**

1.1 Congressman _____ beat Senator _____ with a cane over a speech the senator made.

1.2 The three candidates in the 1856 election were _____ , _____ , and _____ .

1.3 One of the last united political institutions in 1855 was the _____ Party.

1.4 The Lecompton Constitution was supported in Washington by _____ , but was successfully opposed by _____ .

1.5 The anti-slavery movement seriously took off in the decade of the _____ .

1.6 The main source of livelihood in the South was _____ .

1.7 Buchanan's policies tended to favor the _____ .

1.8 Pro-slavery partisans looted and burned the town of _____ , Kansas in 1856.

1.9 By 1857 most of the people in Kansas were _____- slavery.

1.10 The speech that got Charles Sumner into trouble was entitled "_____ ."

1.11 _____ murdered five pro-slavery men in Pottawatomie Creek in response to the invasion of Lawrence.

1.12 The Republican slogan in 1856 was _____ .

Answer these questions.

1.13 What made the South think the North was a threat to their way of life?

_____
_____
_____

1.14 How had the Democrats and Whigs dealt with the slavery issue before 1855?

_____

1.15 What was wrong with the Lecompton Constitution?

_____
_____
_____

1.16 Why did Kansas become known as "Bleeding Kansas?"

_____

_____

1.17 Why was Buchanan chosen as the Democratic candidate in 1856?

_____

_____

Dred Scott Decision. The tense situation in 1857 was **exacerbated** by the decision of the Supreme Court in _Dred Scott v. Sandford_. Dred Scott was an enslaved man who had lived for five years in the North with his master. He sued for his freedom on the basis of his long residence on free soil. It was a test case financed by abolitionists. It eventually reached the Supreme Court.

The Supreme Court of 1857 had nine justices, five from the South. Seven of the justices were Democrats, and two were Republicans. The Chief Justice, Roger Taney, was a Southerner and wrote the opinion of the court. The court ruled that Scott was not a citizen and could not sue in federal court. That is all the court needed to rule to end the case; unfortunately, it went further. Taney ruled that Scott was not free. He was considered property protected under the Fifth Amendment. It was therefore unconstitutional for the federal government to bar slavery _anywhere_ in the United States!

The **repercussions** of the decision were vast. At one stroke, the Supreme Court claimed all of the country to be slave territory. Popular sovereignty no longer applied because people could not vote to keep constitutionally-protected slaves out of their states. All of the compromises to limit the spread of slavery were in one swoop declared unconstitutional. The court made a political decision based on its own prejudices.

The South rejoiced at the decision. The North swore to defy it, justifiably believing that it was a political decision by a Southern-dominated court that went beyond the issues of the case. Northern Democrats who supported popular sovereignty were now forced farther away from their Southern counterparts who supported the Dred Scott decision. Southerners were alarmed by the voices in the North that threatened to defy the courts and deny slave owners protection for their "property." The decision widened the North-South rift still further.

Panic of 1857. The nation was struck with one of its periodic depressions in 1857. Businesses had over-extended themselves during a boom time by speculating in land and railroads. The collapse closed thousands of businesses and caused widespread unemployment. It hit the manufacturing and grain-growing sections of the nation the hardest. The South rode out the panic comfortably because of the high international demand for cotton. Southerners saw the entire depression as proof of their superior way of life.

The Panic of 1857 created a clamor for higher tariffs in the North. Tariffs had been lowered in order to please the South. Northerners resented what they saw as a Southern blockade on Northern prosperity. Thus, the depression contributed to the division in the nation.

Lincoln-Douglas Debates. Democratic Senator Stephen Douglas was up for re-election in 1858. His Republican opponent was a tall, thin, back-country lawyer named Abraham Lincoln. Lincoln challenged Douglas to a series of debates which were held all over Illinois. Because of the prominence of Douglas and the growing reputation of Lincoln, the debates drew nationwide attention.

Douglas had a substantial advantage in the election. He was a well-known figure with several years of experience in Washington and an excellent orator. In Illinois he had redeemed himself for the Kansas-Nebraska Act by his opposition to the Lecompton Constitution. Illinois still generally favored popular sovereignty which was Douglas' primary position. In contrast, Lincoln had only served one term in the House of Representatives at the national level and had a high, thin voice. His Republican party was considered a threat to the Union in the South. Northern voters took that into consideration.

However, Lincoln was passionate about his subject and addressed the issues in clear, honest terms. He openly stated that he believed slavery was morally wrong. He did not believe it could be constitutionally ended where it already existed, but the spread of it should be prevented at all costs. He challenged Douglas on the issue of popular sovereignty, saying that slavery was an issue for the entire nation, not just the people who happened to move to a territory before a specific date. Moreover, Douglas and popular sovereignty denied the moral issues entirely, treating slavery and slaves as just another choice for voters. Lincoln also asked how Douglas could support popular sovereignty in the light of the Dred Scott decision, which stripped it of all constitutional support.

Douglas responded with a mix of politics and reasoning. He pointedly poked fun at Lincoln's lack of political experience and his background as a working man. He accused Lincoln of

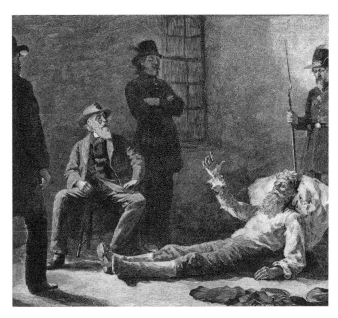

| The capture of John Brown, depicted by an early sketch artist

favoring equality between black and white people (a charge which Lincoln refuted). Douglas also argued that even with the Dred Scott decision, popular sovereignty still had force. He said that slavery could not exist without state laws to protect slaves as property. Therefore, when states refused to pass such laws, slavery could not safely exist there, even if constitutional.

Douglas won the senate race, but the debates cost him his chance at the presidency. Newspapers had printed the texts of the debates all over the nation. Southern voters read about Douglas' proposal for states to annul Dred Scott by not passing the state laws needed to protect slavery. That proposal cost Douglas his support in the South. Lincoln was upset by the loss but he accepted it as "a slip, not a fall." The debates had made him a national Republican figure.

Harper's Ferry Raid. After the murders in Kansas at Pottawatomie Creek, John Brown and much of his family had fled to Canada. From there, he planned a grand attack on slavery. His scheme was to invade the South, seize weapons, lead the slaves in a revolt, and set up stronghold sanctuaries for black people in

| Abolitionist John Brown

| Stephen Douglas

the South. From these strongholds, he would organize an army to overrun the South. He chose to begin by attacking the federal **arsenal** at Harper's Ferry, Virginia.

In October of 1859, Brown and about twenty men captured the arsenal, taking several hostages. They held the building for over a day and killed several people. The black people that Brown had expected to rally to his aid never came. Instead, a detachment of federal troops arrived under the command of Colonel Robert E. Lee. Brown was quickly captured and most of his men with him.

John Brown's trial for treason drew phenomenal national attention. Brown behaved in a brave and dignified manner during the trial. His courageous devotion to freedom made many abolitionists overlook his violent nature and methods. Brown showed many signs of insanity, and it would have been wise to confine him to an asylum. Instead he was quickly tried, found guilty, and hanged. His death made him a martyr for the anti-slavery cause.

Brown gained a reputation in death that he never had in life. Abolitionists ignored his past and hailed him as a saint. There were

demonstrations throughout the North on the day he was executed. A popular song was written about him that became a marching song in the Civil War. It ran, in part:

*John Brown's body lies a-moul'ring
in the grave,
His soul is marching on.*

The raid made the South even more suspicious of the North. Many knowledgeable moderates condemned Brown and his methods, but the South saw the public support for this murderous man and believed that was the direction the North was headed itself. The division grew.

The Election of 1860. The Democratic Party finally split over the issue of slavery in 1860. The party was unable to name a candidate at their first convention. A second convention was held and the Southern states walked out, as they had at the first. The Northern Democrats then nominated Stephen Douglas. Douglas ran on a platform of popular sovereignty and strict enforcement of the Fugitive Slave Act. The Southern Democrats met at their own convention and nominated John C. Breckinridge of Kentucky. Breckinridge campaigned on the basis of enforcing the Dred Scott Decision.

To add to the confusion, a group of Know-Nothings and Whigs formed a middle-of-the-road Constitutional Union Party and nominated John Bell of Tennessee.

The Republicans had a clear chance at victory with their opposition divided three ways. They nominated Abraham Lincoln over the better-known William Seward because Lincoln was less controversial. The Republicans also created a platform to keep themselves from being a one-issue party. The platform included:

protective tariffs for the North, federal money for internal improvements for the west, free homesteads for farmers, a Northern railroad across the nation for the northwest, protection of the rights of immigrants, and its primary stand, no extension of slavery into the territories. Lincoln won the election, taking almost all the electoral votes in the North along with Oregon and California. However, in the popular vote he won just under 40%, making him a minority president.

 Answer these questions.

1.18 Why did Dred Scott argue he should be free?

_____

1.19 What did John Brown attack in 1859?

_____

1.20 Who commanded the troops that captured Brown?

_____

1.21 What caused the Panic of 1857?

_____

1.22 What made Lincoln a national figure?

_____

1.23 What was the only necessary part of the ruling in the Dred Scott case?

_____

1.24 What was the unnecessary and controversial part of the Dred Scott decision?

_____

_____

1.25 How did Douglas defend the idea of popular sovereignty after Dred Scott?

_____

_____

1.26 What happened to John Brown after his raid into Virginia?

_____

1.27 Name the candidates and their parties in the 1860 election.

a. _____

b. _____

c. _____

d. _____

1.28 What was the constitutional effect of the Dred Scott decision?

_____

1.29 What was Lincoln's opinion of slavery and what to do about it?

_____

_____

1.30 What happened to John Brown's reputation after his death?

_____

1.31 What were the proposals of the Republican platform in 1860?

a. _____

b. _____

c. _____

d. _____

e. _____

f. _____

1.32 Why did each of the following increase the South's desire to separate from the North?

Dred Scott

a. _____

_____

Panic of 1857

b. _____

_____

John Brown's raid

c. _____

_____

Secession

The South Secedes. There were four long months between the time Lincoln was elected in November of 1860 and the day he became president in March of 1861. The South took full advantage of the lull. Convinced that its unique and superior culture could not survive under a hated Republican president, South Carolina called a special constitutional convention in December of 1860. The Convention voted to secede from the Union. Six other states from the deep South quickly followed suit.

The seven states met together in February of 1861 and formed their own government. They called themselves the Confederate States of America or the Confederacy. They elected Jefferson Davis of Mississippi as president of the new "nation." The capital was established at Montgomery, Alabama. (It was later moved to Richmond, Virginia when that state seceded.)

President James Buchanan, with his pro-South advisors, was no match for the crisis. He made several speeches that accomplished nothing. He essentially said that a state could not secede, but that the federal government had no power to stop it if it did! He refused to strengthen the garrisons at federal forts in the South, as was recommended by the elderly General Winfield Scott. He did try to send reinforcements to Fort Sumter in South Carolina, but the effort was inadequate and the troops were forced to return.

Crittenden Compromise. As the crises matured, several attempts were made to work out a compromise. The most promising was a series of constitutional amendments proposed by Senator John Crittenden of Kentucky. The Crittenden Compromise would have guaranteed the protection of slavery where it already existed. It would have barred slavery in the territories north of the Missouri Compromise line of 36° 30' and protected it in all territories, present or future, south of it. Any states formed

| A modern photo of Fort Sumter

in the Southern territories would have popular sovereignty on the subject. The compromise failed because Lincoln was loyal to his beliefs and his party's platform. He refused to consider allowing slavery in the territories. It might have failed anyway, given the control the radicals had in the Confederate States.

In the end, the South seceded without any opposition from Buchanan. Most Southerners believed the North would never fight. The Northern factories needed Southern cotton too badly. Southern pride would not allow them to consider the possibility that the factory workers, shopkeepers, and fishermen of the North could put up any serious opposition. Pride went before the fall.

Abraham Lincoln. Abraham Lincoln (1809-1865) was one of the greatest men ever to occupy the presidency. He was born to a poor family in Kentucky. His family later moved to Indiana and then Illinois. Abe, as he was known, was a strong man who spent most of his youth working with his hands. His political propaganda called him the "Rail Splitter" for all the logs he had split over the years to make fences.

He had very little formal education (maybe a year) yet he loved to read, often walking miles to borrow a book. He failed in business and eventually got into law and politics in Illinois.

Abraham Lincoln entered the presidency with deceptively poor qualifications. He had served four terms in the Illinois House of Representatives and one in the U.S. House. Those were his only political qualifications. Yet, Lincoln had also been a popular Whig and Republican speaker in Illinois. He knew how to organize and administer political power. He had learned how to express himself in speech-making and in the courtroom in a way that persuaded his listeners. He had a reputation for integrity that earned him the nickname "Honest Abe." He had a strong will and the strength of convictions. Moreover, he was no Buchanan. He was willing to put force behind his beliefs and would accept the consequences.

Lincoln was sworn in on March 3, 1861. He tried to steer a moderate path in his inaugural address. He denied any intention of interfering with slavery where it already existed. There would be no conflict unless the South started one. He was still hoping to avoid a war, but he made it clear he would defend the Union. The South could not simply pull out because it did not like the outcome of a fairly contested election, for that made a mockery of democracy.

Fort Sumter. Fort Sumter was one of the few Southern federal forts still in Union hands when Lincoln became president. It was located at the mouth of the harbor for the city of Charleston, South Carolina. The fort's commander, Robert Anderson, steadfastly refused Southern demands to surrender his command, but his supplies were running low. Lincoln knew that sending reinforcements to the fort would touch off a strong reaction in that state. In the end, he compromised. He sent a boatload of provisions, but no new troops.

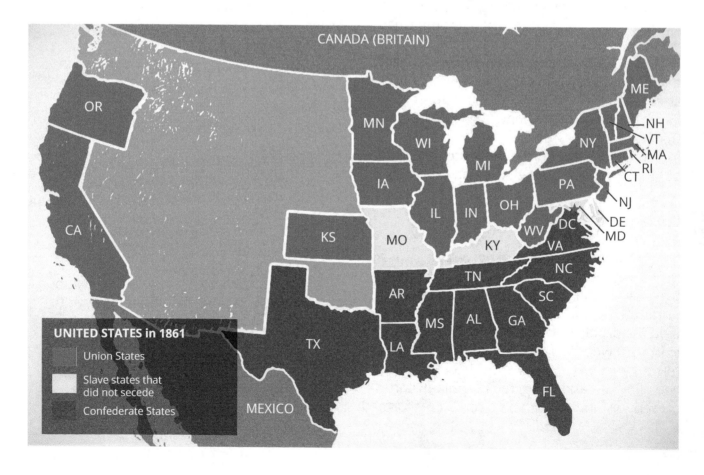

UNITED STATES in 1861

- Union States
- Slave states that did not secede
- Confederate States

South Carolina was notified of the delivery of the provisions. Its leaders chose to interpret it as an aggressive act. Before the relief ship could arrive, the Carolinians decided to act. On April 12, 1861, under the command of General Pierre Beauregard, the cannons in the city opened fire on the fort. The garrison surrendered the next day.

The attack on Fort Sumter was the official beginning of the Civil War. It united the North in favor of war. Lincoln immediately called for volunteers to put down the rebellion. More men responded than the army could supply. Lincoln also suspended civil rights in areas that had Southern sympathizers. He ordered a blockade of Southern ports, and he ordered federal funds spent to support the war without Congressional approval (Congress was not in session). These actions were arguably unconstitutional, but they were in line with the extraordinary powers used by presidents in wartime. Without a strong, immediate action, there might not have been any country to uphold the Constitution.

The greatest area of concern was the border states. Four of these, Arkansas, Tennessee, North Carolina, and Virginia, seceded once they realized the North would fight to force them to stay in the Union. The northwest counties of Virginia did not vote for secession. The people in these counties seceded from Virginia and formed a new state that was loyal to the Union. West Virginia was admitted to the United States in 1863. The other border/slave states, Missouri, Kentucky, Maryland, and Delaware, stayed in the Union. However, Maryland was kept in by a declaration of martial law by Lincoln. He could not risk having Washington D.C. cut off from the rest of the nation. Thus, the sides were drawn—eleven to twenty-three.

 Complete these sentences.

1.33 The Southern attack on _____ began the Civil War.

1.34 Seven states seceded after the election of Republican candidate

_____ .

1.35 After the war began, _____ more states seceded.

1.36 The most serious attempt to prevent the secession of the South was the

_____ Compromise.

1.37 _____ was president of the United States when the

Confederacy was organized.

1.38 The slave states that stayed in the Union were _____ ,

_____ , _____ ,

and _____ .

1.39 Because of his integrity, Abraham Lincoln was nicknamed _____

_____ .

1.40 _____ was the first state to secede.

1.41 The actions taken by Lincoln as commander-in-chief when the war began included

a. _____ , b. _____ ,

c. _____ , and d. _____ .

1.42 Lincoln's national political experience was limited to one term in the _____

_____ .

1.43 Lincoln sent _____ to Fort Sumter in 1861.

1.44 The Confederate states elected _____ as president.

1.45 The two Confederate capitals were _____ and

_____ .

1.46 The western counties of Virginia formed a new state called _____

and joined the Union in _____ .

Facing Off

Northern Advantages. The North had significant advantages in the Civil War. Money was needed to pursue a war, and the North had four-fifths of the available capital in the nation. The North also had a larger population, 22 million to the South's 9 million (including the 3.5 million slaves). The North had more of the raw materials needed for war, such as coal and iron. Moreover, the North had more factories, farms, and railroads.

Railroads were vital, being used to move troops and supplies. The South was hampered because it never had the resources to build tracks during the war. In order to repair damaged tracks or lay new ones, they had to tear up old ones.

The North controlled the navy and had more ships for moving supplies, so the Union was able to blockade the South. This cut off imports of badly needed manufactured goods. It prevented the South from selling its cotton, which robbed them of their primary income. The blockade eventually led to severe shortages of basic supplies to the South, which hampered

their war effort. While the South was cut off from trade with Europe, the Union was not. Throughout the war, the North was able to sell grain and purchase military equipment by trading with Europe.

| A Northern railroad train, one of the Union's advantages

The Northern armies were eventually augmented by black soldiers. Black men formed one-tenth of the total Union troops by the end of the war. They served in **segregated** companies, led by white officers. They were paid less than white soldiers for part of the war. The South refused to recognize them as prisoners of war, treating them as escaped slaves. In spite of this, black volunteers fought courageously and were a dependable asset to the Union. On the other hand, the South would not even consider employing black soldiers until the very last, desperate days of the war.

The North had the advantage of an established government led by a strong president. Lincoln was an excellent leader whose authority was sustained by a government backed with eighty years of success. By contrast, the South had no united history to sustain them. Their entire government was built on the idea of states' rights and secession from another government. Jefferson Davis had difficulty maintaining his authority over the independent-minded Southern states.

Problems with central authority and the blockade made it difficult for the South to raise money for war. The states' rights Confederacy did not favor taxes, and the banks had little to offer in loans. The Confederate government printed money to pay its bills, which pushed up prices to many, many times what they were at the beginning of the war. The inflation added to Southern difficulties in prosecuting a war.

Southern Advantages. The South had some of the advantages the original thirteen colonies did during the War for Independence. In terms of ideals, the Rebels were fighting for independence and protecting their way of life. The North initially did not fight to end slavery, but only to preserve the Union by forcing the South to stay. Strategically, the South only had to survive to win. Southerners could fight a defensive war, protecting their homes and land. The North had to conquer the entire South and force it back into the Union. A simple draw would be a Confederate victory.

| Union soldiers

The South also had better quality officers than were available in the North. The gentlemen of the South had a long tradition of military training and service. Robert E. Lee, for example, had been an officer in the U.S. Army when the war began. He resigned when his home state of Virginia seceded and rose quickly to become the leader of the Confederate army. Other talented Southern officers included Thomas (Stonewall) Jackson, James Longstreet, and Jeb Stuart.

By contrast, the North did not have as many high-quality military leaders. The Northern generals seemed to be either overly cautious or foolhardy. Lincoln changed his commanders several times before he found a successful general in Ulysses S. Grant.

The Confederacy began the war with high hopes. They sincerely believed in the superiority of their way of life and their people. They did not believe the North would fight. Even if they did, no Northern shopkeeper could stand in a fight with a Southern gentleman. They expected that the North and Europe needed Southern cotton. If the North proved to be stubborn, Europe would be likely to intervene on behalf of the South to protect its own textile industries.

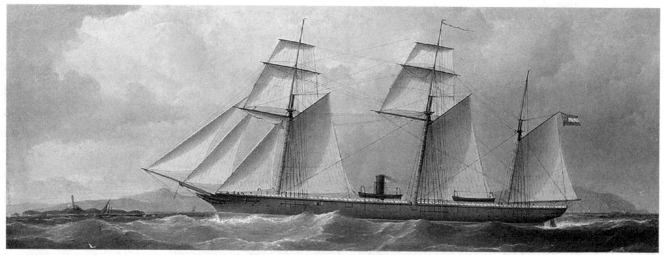

On July 29, 1862, Hull "No. 290" steamed out of the Mersey from the Laird's Birkenhead Yard and into Civil War history. Soon taking her given name, ALABAMA, the Commerce Raider set out on a tour with devastating results for the American North's commercial shipping interests the world over. The screw sloop-of-war proved to be a fast, capable ship under the command of Captain Raphael Semmes, capturing or destroying 69 ships in less than two years.

Reactions Abroad. The best chance for the Confederacy lay in gaining support from the nations of Europe. The monarchs of Europe had good reason to want to see the United States divided. The failure of the American democratic experiment would strengthen the hand of the European aristocrats. These same aristocrats had a natural preference for the class-conscious culture of the South. Moreover, an independent Confederacy would be a supplier for European factories and a purchaser of European goods without the protective tariffs of the North.

English manufacturers were particularly dependent upon Southern cotton to supply their spindles and looms. The blockade threw thousands of textile workers out of their jobs. However, at the same time, the North was supplying much of Britain's wheat and corn. Britain would have had to risk its food supply if it supported the Confederacy for the sake of its cotton supply. Also, cotton suppliers in India and Egypt stepped up production to fill the need. Union demands for war goods also helped relieve employment problems. Thus, Britain was never pushed to intervene by the problems in its economy.

Britain did come very close to war over an incident in the fall of 1861, however. An American warship stopped a British steamer, the *Trent*, leaving the West Indies. Two passengers were arrested and taken back to the U.S. The men were Confederate diplomats en route to Europe. The British government was furious over this seizure of civilian passengers and threatened war. The incident was settled by releasing the men along with a U.S. statement **disavowing** their capture.

There was nevertheless a strong pro-Confederacy attitude in the British government at the beginning of the war. The government considered recognizing the Confederate nation especially when the South garnered a string of victories early in the war. Many ships for the Confederate navy were built in Britain during the war. Careful Union diplomacy limited this activity. What destroyed all hope of both British and French aid to the Confederacy was the Emancipation Proclamation in 1862. Once the war was reframed as a fight against slavery, neither of the great powers of Europe would raise their hands to aid the South. Thus, the aid the U.S. had during the Revolution was denied to the Confederacy in the Civil War.

Put an *N* beside the factors that were an advantage for the North and an *S* beside those that were an advantage for the South.

1.47 _____ ideals at the beginning of the war

1.48 _____ population

1.49 _____ manufacturing

1.50 _____ military personnel

1.51 _____ strategic position

1.52 _____ government

1.53 _____ navy

1.54 _____ hope for foreign allies

1.55 _____ black soldiers

1.56 _____ capital

1.57 _____ military tradition

1.58 _____ railroads

1.59 _____ farms

Answer these questions.

1.60 What effect did the blockade have on the South? _____

_____

_____

1.61 Why did the nations of Europe tend to favor the South? _____

_____

_____

1.62 What did the North provide for Britain that offset the loss of Southern cotton?

_____

_____

1.63 What happened in the *Trent* incident? _____

_____

_____

_____

1.64 What ended all hope of European aid to the Confederacy?

_____

↺ **Review the material in this section in preparation for the Self Test.** The Self Test will check your mastery of this particular section. The items missed on this Self Test will indicate specific areas where restudy is needed for mastery.

SELF TEST 1

Match these people (each answer, 2 points).

1.01	_____ John Brown	a. Confederate general
1.02	_____ James Buchanan	b. violent abolitionist martyr
1.03	_____ Abraham Lincoln	c. beaten by a Congressman in the U.S. Senate
1.04	_____ Stephen Douglas	d. offered a compromise after secession
1.05	_____ Charles Sumner	e. first Republican presidential candidate
1.06	_____ Dred Scott	f. slave who lived in the North and sued for his freedom
1.07	_____ Robert E. Lee	g. U.S. president when the Confederacy began
1.08	_____ Jefferson Davis	h. president of the Confederacy
1.09	_____ John Frémont	i. his election prompted Southern secession
1.010	_____ John Crittenden	j. won the 1858 senate race in Illinois

Choose the correct word(s) to complete each sentence (each answer, 3 points).

1.011 Twisted, illegal version of popular sovereignty produced the pro-slavery _____ Constitution in Kansas.

1.012 The _____ Party opposed the spread of slavery but agreed it could not be abolished where it already existed.

1.013 The Civil War began when Confederate forces fired on _____ .

1.014 John Brown was executed for his attack on the arsenal at _____ , Virginia.

1.015 The _____ - _____ Debates centered on the issue of slavery and made Abraham Lincoln a national figure.

1.016 The Supreme Court declared that slavery was legal in all of the U.S. in the

_____ Decision.

1.017 The South had little difficulty with the Panic of 1857 because of the high price of

_____ on the international market.

1.018 The era of compromise was ended by the _____ - _____ Act.

1.019 _____ was the first state to secede.

1.020 Any hope of European aid to the Confederacy was ended by the

_____ .

Complete these items (each answer, 3 points).

1.021 Name four advantages the North had in the Civil War.

a. _____   b. _____

c. _____   d. _____

1.022 Name two advantages the South had at the beginning of the war.

a. _____   b. _____

1.023 Give two reasons why the nations of Europe might have supported the South.

a. _____   b. _____

1.024 Name two border/slave states that did not secede.

a. _____   b. _____

Answer true or false (each answer, 2 points).

1.025 _____ Abraham Lincoln believed that the U.S. could not continue to be part slave and part free.

1.026 _____ Britain almost went to war with the Union after two Confederate officials were arrested on the British steamer the _Trent_.

1.027 _____ The South received a tremendous number of immigrants in the years leading up to the Civil War.

1.028 _____ The Democratic Party split in two in 1860.

1.029 _____ James Buchanan did little to solve the divisions in the nation.

1.030 _____ Black soldiers in the Union army served in segregated units, usually with white officers.

1.031 _____ The blockade of the South hurt textile manufacturers in Britain.

1.032 _____ Abraham Lincoln was a well-educated man with many years of national experience when he became president.

1.033 _____ Lincoln believed slavery was morally wrong.

1.034 _____ The American abolitionist movement began its serious growth in the 1830s.

80 / 100   SCORE _____   TEACHER _____ _____
initials   date

| Painting by Civil War artist Dale Gallon

2. CIVIL WAR

The horrors of the Civil War were its nature and its cost. It was a *civil war*, fought between countrymen, friends, and family. Many of the opposing army officers had served together in the Mexican War. It was not uncommon for relatives to be on opposing sides. Senator John Crittenden, whose name is attached to the compromise, had sons who fought on opposite sides. One Union navy officer boarded a captured ship only to find his dead Confederate son aboard. Abraham Lincoln's sister-in-law was married to a Confederate general. She came to live in the White House for a time after her husband was killed in the war. It was a very personal war.

It was also a very bloody war. More Americans died in the Civil War than in World War I, Korea, or Vietnam. Only World War II cost America more lives. In fact, all the battle deaths in all the other wars before World War II added together does not equal the total from this "family conflict."

An estimated 620,000 died in battle and from disease and accidents (figures from the Civil War Trust). Thousands lost legs, arms, and/or their health.

The reason for the bloodshed was an advancement in technology without an appropriate change in military thinking. Since its invention, the soldier's firearm had been an inaccurate, slow-firing musket. By the 1860s, faster firing, very accurate rifles were in general use and artillery was improving. Standard military tactics, based on the older weapons, would send large numbers of men to attack enemy positions even if they had built barricades to protect themselves. The weapons were so poor that an attacking army had a good chance of overrunning an enemy position if it had enough men. The newer weapons made such attacks suicidal. However, all of the Civil War commanders only knew the old mass-attack tactics and used them to the bitter end.

SECTION OBJECTIVES

Review these objectives. When you have completed this section, you should be able to:

4. List the advantages of both sides in the Civil War.

5. Describe the major battles and the course of the Civil War.

7. Describe the background and policies of Civil War-era presidents.

VOCABULARY

Study these words to enhance your learning success in this section.

amputate (am' pyu tāt). To cut off, especially a limb of a person.

anesthetic (an' es thet' ik). A substance that cause a loss of feeling in all or part of the body.

chaplain (chap len). A member of the clergy serving in a special group or place, like a prison or the military.

conscription (kon skrip' shun). Forced enrollment of people, mostly for military service.

division (di vizh' in). A large military unit that has all the necessary services to work as a self-contained unit and act independently.

morale (mo ral'). Moral or mental condition in regard to courage, confidence, or enthusiasm.

repulse (ri puls'). To drive back; repel.

Bull Run to Fredericksburg (1861-62)

First Bull Run. After Fort Sumter in April of 1861, Lincoln called for the state militia to come into service for three months. By May he realized the ill-trained, short-term militia would not be enough. A new call was put out for volunteers for a three-year enlistment. By summer, thousands of men were being organized into an army near Washington. A similar call had been made in the Confederacy, and its army was forming in Virginia near Richmond. The two capitals and their respective armies were only 120 miles apart.

Winfield Scott, the old commander of the U.S. army, wanted a slow, steady strategy to defeat the South. His plan called for a naval blockade to strangle Southern ports and the Mississippi River. In the meantime, the army would cut the South into pieces. This basic plan was the one followed by the Union throughout the war, even after Scott retired because of poor health. Scott wanted to take the time to drill and prepare the very untried Union troops before mounting any attacks, but the president and the American public were too impatient to wait.

Lincoln pressed the new Union field commander, Irvin McDowell, to attack at once. McDowell argued that his troops were untrained and not ready, but Lincoln prevailed. In July, the Union army moved south to attack the Confederacy. On July 21st, under the command of General Joe Johnston, the Union army met the Confederates near a creek called Bull Run and a town called Manassas Junction. The Northern public was convinced that it would be an easy victory. Many of the people of Washington brought picnic lunches and drove out to watch what they thought would be the only battle of the war.

The battle was a disaster for the Union. The green troops fought well at first, but as the equally green Confederate lines began to break, General Thomas Jackson stood his ground. A Confederate colleague yelled for the men to fight behind Jackson who was standing "like a stone wall." Jackson thus earned a

| The aftermath of First Bull Run

nickname (Stonewall) and the beginning of a famous reputation as a general. Confederate reinforcements arrived, and it was the Union lines that began to break. The North retreated and then ran in disarray. However the disorganized, untrained Confederates failed to follow up on the Union defeat. Both armies were left intact.

The defeat cleared up Union hopes of keeping the war short. The Union began the difficult preparations for a long war, but no one had any idea how long and difficult it would actually be. In the meantime, the South was delighted with the victory, which they saw as a vindication of their superiority. They did not expect a long war and became overconfident.

McClellan in Charge. McDowell was replaced by George McClellan. McClellan proved to be an excellent organizer. He trained and drilled the Union army for months. He also built up defenses around Washington to protect the capital from any enemy attack. He built a professional, well-organized, well-supplied army which was named the Army of the Potomac.

However, McClellan was cautious to the point of near cowardice. He refused to attack until he had everything where he wanted it and believed he had a large numerical advantage. As Lincoln so aptly put it, McClellan had a "case of the slows."

Forts Henry and Donelson. The Union strategy in the west was to gain control of the Mississippi River and its major tributaries. That would give the Union firm control of the border states of Missouri and Kentucky as well as a dominant position in Tennessee. It would cut off Louisiana, Arkansas, and Texas from the rest of the Confederacy. Attacks from the North were under the command of General Ulysses S. Grant. Grant had been out of the army for several years before the war and had a reputation for drinking that haunted his whole career,

but he was a fighter. He promptly went after two key river forts near the Tennessee-Kentucky border.

Fort Henry on the Tennessee River fell quickly to Grant and his supporting navy gunboats on February 6th of 1862. Nearby Fort Donelson on the Cumberland River was more difficult. The fort's better guns badly damaged the Union navy ships, but Grant managed to get his troops around the forts and set up a siege. The garrison tried, but was unable to break out and on February the 16th, the Confederate commander asked for terms of surrender. U.S. Grant insisted that nothing "except unconditional and immediate surrender can be accepted." The Confederates complied, and the Union general won the nickname "Unconditional Surrender" Grant.

| Battles for control of the Mississippi

The fall of the forts led the Confederate army to evacuate Nashville which then fell into Union hands. It was the first captured state capital. This was welcome news to victory-hungry President Lincoln and the Union. It made Grant a hero. More good news came in April with the capture of Island Number Ten, a heavily fortified Confederate position near where the Ohio and Mississippi Rivers met.

Shiloh. Grant promptly moved south after the victory at Donelson to Pittsburg Landing on the Tennessee River. He was headed for Corinth, an important railroad junction 22 miles away. Grant failed to prepare any defenses, believing the Confederates would not attack. However, they did attack on April 6th near a hill called Shiloh and caught the Union army by surprise.

The Battle of Shiloh lasted for two days. It was a confused and vicious fight. Many soldiers mistakenly fired on their own troops. Confederate commander Albert Johnston was killed. Union men took cover in a sunken road and slaughtered their Confederate attackers. The Southern army responded by raining artillery on the immobilized Union troops. The field caught fire, burning many of the wounded to death. The Union lines held, however, and reinforcements arriving the next day forced the Confederates to retreat.

About 4,000 Americans died in the two days of the Battle of Shiloh, and more would die later due to their wounds. The total of the casualties (dead or wounded) was around 13,000 from the Union and 10,000 from the Confederacy. Grant's exhausted, victorious army could not even follow the retreating rebels, who were allowed to escape. The bloodshed shocked both the North and South. Lincoln was pressured to fire Grant, but he said, "I can't spare this man—he fights."

| Admiral David Farragut

New Orleans. Admiral David Farragut led a federal naval attack on New Orleans in April. The city was the largest in the South and a key port for the entire Mississippi River. It was protected by two huge forts in the harbor. At first, Farragut tried to batter the forts into submission. Once that failed, he decided to slip by them at night. He lost only one boat in the attempt, and with the city at his mercy, New Orleans surrendered.

In May, Farragut headed up the Mississippi to capture the capital of Louisiana, Baton Rouge. Meanwhile, General Henry Halleck took over active command of Grant's forces while the latter was in temporary disgrace. Halleck marched south, forcing the Confederate army to evacuate Corinth. In June the Union navy forced the surrender of Memphis. Only the fortress city of Vicksburg, Mississippi (in between Farragut and Halleck) kept the Union from complete control of the nation's largest river system.

Complete the following.

2.1 Explain why there were so many battle casualties in the Civil War.

_____

_____

2.2 What were the positive results of McClellan's command?

_____

_____

_____

2.3 Why was McClellan not a good field commander?

_____

_____

2.4 Name the only American war to date that caused more deaths than the Civil War.

_____

2.5 According to the *World Almanac*, how many Americans died in battle and from disease and

accidents in the Civil War? _____

Name the battle or place.

2.6 _____ "Stonewall" Jackson got his nickname

2.7 _____ "Unconditional Surrender" Grant got his nickname

2.8 _____ Admiral Farragut sailed his ships past the harbor forts at night

2.9 _____ Irvin McDowell was the Union commander

2.10 _____ green Confederate troops routed green Union troops

2.11 _____ fort on the Tennessee River fell easily to Grant

2.12 _____ Bloody battle cost 23,000 Union and Confederate casualties

2.13 _____ Washington citizens took picnic lunches out to watch

2.14 _____ the fall of these two forts set up the Union occupation of Nashville

2.15 _____ Grant was surprised by the Confederates at Pittsburg Landing

2.16 _____ important railroad junction, the goal of Grant after Donelson

2.17 _____ defeat that made the Union realize it would not be an easy war

2.18 _____ Lincoln and public opinion forced a Union attack with untrained troops against the wishes of the commander

Battle of the Ironclads. The Union's blockade of the South developed slowly. The North captured several key islands along the Southern coast early in the war to use as bases for the blockade fleet. But the thousands of miles of Southern coast could not all be watched. Eventually, the navy began to concentrate on the few Southern ports that had dock facilities to handle cotton bales, the South's currency in trade. This and the eventual capture of these ports made the blockade increasingly effective.

The South countered by using fast, dark-colored ships to run the blockade. The ships would take cotton from the South to British ports in the West Indies to trade for manufactured goods. The demand for luxury items in the South made the risky voyages very profitable. A ship owner could make a profit if his vessel made just two successful trips before it was captured. Eventually, Jefferson Davis' government insisted that half of all cargo space on the ships be used for war material, not silks and perfume.

The South tried to break the blockade. They almost succeeded, using the captured Union steamship *Merrimac*. When the Union withdrew from Norfolk Navy Yard shortly after the outset of the Civil War, the Union Navy sank the *Merrimac* to keep it from falling into enemy hands. The Confederates recovered and salvaged the steam-powered ship, and modified it by covering it with iron plates. They rearmed and renamed the ship the *Virginia* and used it with devastating effect to attack the wooden ships that blockaded Chesapeake Bay. The Union ships' cannon fire bounced harmlessly off of the steel-covered ship.

Fortunately, the Union had also developed an ironclad vessel. The *Monitor* arrived in time to confront the *Virginia* when it made its second appearance in the bay. The two ships fought an inconclusive four-hour battle because neither side had developed armor-piercing artillery shells. Out of both ammunition and resolve, the ships returned to their home ports. Eventually, the Union Navy claimed the battle's victory because the blockade was not broken. Later, both ships were lost. The Confederacy destroyed the *Virginia* (*Merrimac*), and the North lost the *Monitor* and its crew in a storm off the coast of Cape Hatteras. The battle of the *Monitor* and the *Merrimac* was the first battle in history to be fought between armor-plated ships.

| The *Monitor* and the *Merrimac*

Peninsular Campaign. McClellan had finally agreed to attack in the spring of 1862. He decided against a direct attack to the South. Instead, he had his entire army transported by sea to the peninsula between the York and the James River on Chesapeake Bay in Virginia. He hoped to outflank the Confederates and capture Richmond, which would be about 70 miles from his landing point. Lincoln reluctantly approved the plan, but insisted that a large number of troops be left behind to defend Washington.

McClellan landed safely with more than 100,000 men and in April of 1862 began to march toward Richmond. They confronted the Confederate army under the command of Joe Johnston in the inconclusive two-day battle of Fair Oaks (Seven Pines). Johnston was wounded and Robert E. Lee was given command of the Confederate forces which he called the Army of Northern Virginia.

| Lincoln and McClellan meeting at Antietam

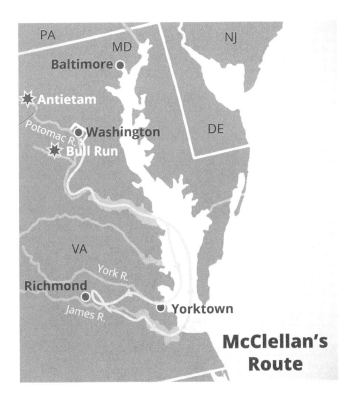

McClellan's Route

Stonewall Jackson used a smaller Confederate force to tie up McClellan's reinforcements around Washington in the Shenandoah Valley. Moving quickly and winning several small battles, Jackson convinced the Union high command that an attack on Washington was taking place. After fighting enough to insure the Union troops would remain there looking for him, Jackson slipped away and joined up with Lee.

Using information gained by Jeb Stuart's cavalry, which made a spectacular ride all the way around McClellan's army, Lee attacked on June 26th. The Seven Days' Battles raged from June 26th to July 1st with a series of savage battles in what are now the suburbs of Richmond. Lee succeeded in forcing McClellan to retreat to the James River. McClellan believed he was hopelessly outnumbered and refused to take the offensive again. He was finally ordered to return his army to Washington in the hopes it could be used from there.

Second Bull Run. While McClellan was in Virginia, the army around Washington was under the command of John Pope. Pope advanced toward Richmond in July, believing that McClellan's army on the peninsula would keep Lee too busy to stop him. But Lee realized the caliber of his opponents. Lee was certain that McClellan would be too busy moving his army to interfere with the Confederate army for a time, so Lee left a small force on the peninsula and led the rest of the army north to deal with Pope before McClellan's troops could join him. Lee sent Jackson to circle around Pope and cut his lines of supply and communication. As Lee expected, Pope turned his army and tried to find Jackson to do battle. Then Lee brought the Army of Northern Virginia to Jackson's aid.

The Battle of Second Bull Run went badly for the Union. Pope was very confused. He had finally cornered Jackson on August 29th after an exhausting search and had attacked him hard. Jackson managed to hold on for that day, and the next day Lee arrived. Pope never knew he was there until the Confederate army attacked from the side (flank). The Union army was routed.

That summer was the beginning of Lee's spectacular reputation as a general. Robert E. Lee was a devout Christian man from an aristocratic, but not very wealthy, Southern family. He gained several properties by his marriage into the family of George Washington's wife. He did not really believe slavery was just, but like so many in his day, he owned slaves and accepted "the institution." He fought for the Confederacy because he would not fight against his home state of Virginia. Most experts agree that he was the best general on either side during the Civil War. As at Second Bull Run, he routinely took chances, and he out-maneuvered and out-fought his Union opponents. By the end of the war, the soldiers of the Confederacy loved him and trusted him completely, even when he was wrong.

Confederate Soldier

Union Soldier

Antietam. Lee decided it was time for the Confederacy to go on the offensive. A rebel victory in Union territory might convince Britain to recognize the Confederacy and convince the North to give up the war. So Lee and his army moved into Maryland, heading for the capital of Pennsylvania. McClellan, whose command had been reduced after the peninsula campaign, was given command again under public pressure. He took his reorganized army out to meet Lee.

Lee divided his army to capture Harper's Ferry and press an attack to the north. McClellan learned of the plans when a lost copy of Lee's orders accidentally got into Union hands, but McClellan did not move fast enough to trap Lee with his army spread out. The two sides met near Antietam Creek on September 17th. It was the single bloodiest day of the long, bloody war. In one day, there were over 20,000 casualties between the two armies. Militarily, the battle was a draw. Lee's lines held but he retreated the next day. History records a Union victory because they took the field.

Emancipation Proclamation. Lincoln's goal had always been to restore the Union, but he began to see that the North needed a more specific, moral war aim—the end of slavery. He was reluctant to act because he did not want to drive the Northern border states into the arms of the Confederacy, but he had decided by the summer of 1862 to make the move. However, he wanted to wait until after a Union victory to make the announcement. Antietam gave him that chance.

On September 22nd, Lincoln issued the Emancipation Proclamation. It declared that all of the slaves in any state still in rebellion on January 1, 1863 would be forever free. It did not affect the slaves in the Northern border states and did not free any slaves until the South was effectively under Northern control. However, the document meant the end of slavery in the U.S. The North now had a moral cause. Britain, which had waged a world-wide campaign against slavery, would not aid the Confederacy to protect it.

Fredericksburg. McClellan was so slow following Lee that Lincoln lost all patience and finally removed him from command in November. He was replaced by Ambrose E. Burnside. The general was a handsome man with thick side whiskers that were thereafter called "side burns" in his honor. He immediately began an offensive, but he would prove as foolhardy as McClellan was hesitant.

Burnside decided to move his army to the east around Lee's right flank and march from there to Richmond. Burnside successfully moved the army and prepared to cross the Rappahannock River opposite the city of Fredericksburg. However, he insisted on waiting for pontoon bridges to cross. They took more than a week to arrive. By that time, Lee's scouts had warned him of the Union's location and he had set up strong defenses on the high ground near the city.

Faced with a strongly entrenched Confederate army, Burnside should have withdrawn to fight somewhere else. Instead, he attacked on December 13th. Wave after wave of Union soldiers were sent up the hill towards the Confederate guns. By the day's end, Union casualties were 13,000. General Lee said after that carnage, "It is well war is so terrible, or we should grow too fond of it."

Burnside's failures prompted Lincoln to again change generals. This time he choose General Joseph Hooker. Hooker had a reputation as a fighter, and he began to rebuild the army during the winter months in preparation for another summer of fighting. By that point, the war was more than a year and a half old. The Union had captured the upper and lower reaches of the Mississippi, but they had been completely unable to use their superior numbers and supplies to penetrate the eastern Confederate defenses. Richmond was still 120 miles away.

Name the person, event, battle, or item.

2.19 _____ freed all enslaved people in any state still in rebellion on January 1, 1863

2.20 _____ McClellan faced Johnston in the Peninsular Campaign

2.21 _____ Union ironclad that fought the *Merrimac* to a draw

2.22 _____ Lee fought using information from Stuart's ride around the Union army

2.23 _____ Lee advanced into Maryland and was almost trapped when his plans were discovered

2.24 _____ Lee trapped Pope before McClellan could come to his aid

2.25 _____ the best general in the Civil War

2.26 _____ it gave the war its single bloodiest day

2.27 _____ Burnside attacked entrenched Confederate positions on the Rappahannock River

2.28 _____ general who circled behind Pope and drew him away from Richmond

2.29 _____ gave the North a moral cause and kept Britain from supporting the Confederacy

2.30 _____ Confederate vessel that almost broke the blockade on Chesapeake Bay

2.31 _____ cotton from the South would be taken here by blockade runners

2.32 _____ Lee became the Confederate commander after Johnston was injured in this battle

2.33 _____ Lee forced McClellan back to the James River and effectively ended the Peninsular Campaign

2.34 _____ this battle gave Lincoln the "victory" he needed to release the Emancipation Proclamation

2.35 _____ Burnside waited too long for pontoon boats

2.36 _____ removed from Union command for not pursuing Lee

Murfreesboro to Chattanooga (1863)

Murfreesboro. The Union army in the west had been spread out to occupy captured territory. As a result, it had been largely ineffective through the end of 1862. A Confederate invasion of Tennessee floundered in October of 1862. A new Union commander, William Rosecrans, pursued the Confederates into southern Tennessee. They met at the Battle of Murfreesboro beginning on December 31, 1862. The battle raged for three days with a one-day break in the middle. The total casualties for both sides were over 20,000 men. The results were inconclusive. The Confederates retreated, and it was six months before that specific Union army took the offensive again.

Vicksburg. Grant was now in charge of an army in Tennessee. At the end of 1862, he headed south for Vicksburg. Vicksburg was a fortified city on a high bluff overlooking a bend in the Mississippi River. If the Union was to control the river, the city had to be taken. After a delay due to the Confederate cavalry destroying his supply depot and one failed first attempt to get around the city's defenses, Grant decided on more direct measures.

Grant fought his way south along the west bank of the Mississippi River. Eventually, he crossed the river below Vicksburg and came at the city from the east, which was the only level entrance. Grant assaulted the city on May 22nd and was **repulsed**. He set up trenches that blocked all entry into the city and then began a siege. His guns bombarded the city non-stop. Federal gunboats trained their fire on the city and kept Grant supplied with everything his army needed. The people of the city moved into caves to protect themselves and were reduced to living on mule, rat, and dog meat.

The result was inevitable. The Confederacy had no army to send to relieve Vicksburg. Believing he would get better terms on Independence Day than any other time all summer, the Confederate commander surrendered on July 4, 1863. The Confederacy had been divided, and now the Union had complete control of the Mississippi River. Grant had proven himself as the kind of determined, aggressive general that Lincoln wanted.

Chancellorsville. Union General Joseph Hooker moved to attack Lee in the spring of 1863. Lee still held his position at Fredericksburg. Hooker tried to move around Lee's army to the west, past their left flank. For some reason, Hooker lost his nerve just as the move was showing signs of success. He retreated to defensive positions at Chancellorsville, west of Fredericksburg.

Lee quickly moved to attack Hooker in what would be one of his greatest victories. Lee's army was about half the size of Hooker's. Nevertheless, Lee divided the Army of Northern Virginia into two parts. Lee's portion attacked from the front while the other part, under Stonewall Jackson, attacked the Union's right flank. The Union army was taken by surprise and the right flank collapsed.

The Battle of Chancellorsville lasted for four days beginning on May 2nd. The Confederates were never able to completely break the Union lines, but they did maul them fiercely. Attacked on two sides, the Union army literally fought for its life. As at Shiloh, the underbrush caught fire, burning many of the wounded to death. Hooker retreated, but the South did not get off unscathed. In the evening while scouting the area for possible night attack, Stonewall Jackson was accidentally shot by friendly fire. He died on May 10th. Lee would never find an adequate replacement for his brilliant subordinate.

| The Ghosts of Gettysburg

Gettysburg. In the early summer Lee headed north again to try for a major victory on Union soil. The cavalry from the two armies clashed near Brandy Station on June 9th. The Confederates took the field, but for the first time the Union cavalry equated itself well against the famous rebel horsemen. Another part of the Southern army captured some badly-needed supplies by defeating the Union garrison at Winchester. In the meantime, Hooker refused to pursue Lee and insisted he must attack Richmond. Lincoln relieved him of command and replaced him with George Meade. Meade was from Pennsylvania, and Lincoln hoped he would prove persistent in chasing Lee, who was now in his home state.

| George Meade

Lee marched north toward Harrisburg with the Union army in pursuit. On July 1, some of Lee's troops came into the town of Gettysburg, Pennsylvania searching for shoes. They were met by an advance force of Meade's army. Both sides called for reinforcements and the crucial three-day-long Battle of Gettysburg had begun.

The Confederates forced the Union troops out of the city on the first day of the battle. The Union troops took up defensive positions on a series of hills outside the city. Their line was shaped like a fish hook. Robert E. Lee now made one of his few mistakes. He tried to drive the Union army, which was larger than his, out of strong defenses on the top of a hill. The Confederates both suffered and inflicted huge losses as they repeatedly attacked the Union lines on the second day.

On the third day, Lee decided to make a frontal attack on the Union army. He ordered General George Pickett to march 13,000 men straight up on the Union position. Pickett's charge was a slaughter. Half the men who marched up that day did not come back. Lee blamed only himself for having asked his men to do the impossible. The next day, the Army of Northern Virginia retreated.

Gettysburg was the turning point of the war. The Confederate army would never again have the strength to mount a major offensive. It would never again threaten the North with invasion. However, Meade failed to follow up his victory. Lee and his army were allowed to escape and continue to protect the Confederacy. The war would continue for almost two more years.

The Union and the Confederacy had over 20,000 casualties each at Gettysburg. The Union built a cemetery on the site. It was dedicated on November 19, 1863. The main speaker addressed the crowd for two hours. Abraham Lincoln spoke for only two minutes, but it was Lincoln's words which were remembered. The Gettysburg Address still rings through the years as one of Lincoln's finest speeches.

Four score and seven years ago, our fathers brought forth upon this continent a new nation: conceived in liberty, and dedicated to the proposition that all men are created equal.

Now we are engaged in a great civil war…testing whether that nation, or any nation so conceived and so dedicated…can long endure. We are met on a great battlefield of that war.

We have come to dedicate a portion of that field as a final resting place for those who here gave their lives that this nation might live. It is altogether fitting and proper that we should do this.

But, in a larger sense, we cannot dedicate…we cannot consecrate… we cannot hallow this ground. The brave men, living and dead, who struggled here have consecrated it, far above our poor power to add or detract. The world will little note, nor long remember, what we say here, but it can never forget what they did here.

It is for us the living, rather, to be dedicated here to the unfinished work which they who fought here have thus far so nobly advanced. It is rather for us to be here dedicated to the great task remaining before us…that from these honored dead we take increased devotion to that cause for which they gave the last full measure of devotion…that we here highly resolve that these dead shall not have died in vain…that this nation, under God, shall have a new birth of freedom…and that government of the people…by the people…for the people…shall not perish from this earth.

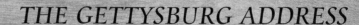

THE GETTYSBURG ADDRESS

Abraham Lincoln, November 19, 1863

Name the battle.

2.37 _____ turning point of the war

2.38 _____ Hooker was defeated by Lee

2.39 _____ Union victory gave them control of the Mississippi

2.40 _____ inconclusive battle in Tennessee under Union leader Rosecrans

2.41 _____ Confederate forces surrendered on the Fourth of July

2.42 _____ four-day battle beginning May 2, 1863

2.43 _____ the opposing armies met when the Confederates came into town looking for shoes

2.44 _____ fought in Pennsylvania

2.45 _____ Grant was unable to win by a direct attack, but won instead by siege

2.46 _____ Pickett's Charge was Lee's last attempt to break the Union lines

2.47 _____ Meade fought Lee

2.48 _____ Lee attacked the Union army from two directions with a smaller army and won

2.49 _____ Stonewall Jackson was shot and later died

2.50 _____ Lincoln's immortal words dedicated a cemetery there

Answer these questions.

2.51 What does "four score and seven years ago" mean? (Look it up.) _____

2.52 Why did Lincoln feel they could not dedicate the cemetery?

_____

_____

2.53 What did Lincoln say he and his listeners must dedicated themselves to do?

_____

2.54 To what was Lincoln highly resolved?

_____

2.55 What did Meade fail to do at Gettysburg that prolonged the war?

_____

_____

The armies. The two opposing armies were at once both similar and different. One important similarity was that both suffered under the limited medical knowledge in the 1860s. The simple idea that a wound should be cleaned to prevent infection was unknown in the mid-19th century. Diseases such as typhoid, dysentery, and pneumonia killed far more soldiers than bullets. The medical treatment for any serious injury to an arm or leg was **amputation**. Treatment was often done without **anaesthetic**. Surgery was usually done with an anaesthetic which had been discovered in the 1840s. However, it was also done with dirty instruments that spread infections.

The North had one advantage in the medical area, determined female volunteers. Northern women established the United States Sanitary Commission in 1861, modeled after the work of the British visionary Florence Nightingale in the Crimean War. The doctors had noticed that a clean camp or hospital resulted in fewer deaths. The Commission worked to provide clean housing for the troops as well as insuring they had ways to bathe and wash their clothes. The Commission also tried to track down missing soldiers and notify families of deaths. The women began to volunteer as nurses in the army hospitals, a revolutionary idea for the time.

The South suffered from a lack of resources to keep its own army clean. As the war progressed, the Confederate army could barely keep its men clothed. It was not surprising that Lee's army was looking for shoes at Gettysburg; they were constantly in need of them. They also lacked uniforms, blankets, soap, and food. The main reason was the poor system of roads and railroads in the South. Even when the supplies were available, it was often impossible to get them to the army in the field.

The Northern army, by contrast, was well-fed and supplied throughout the war. This difference was mainly due to the superior resources of the North. The North had more supplies for its men, and it had better means of transportation to deliver them. The better supplies and cleanliness meant the typical Union soldier was healthier than his Confederate opponent, but poor leadership squandered that and other advantages for most of the war.

Both armies had trouble getting enough soldiers to replace those that deserted, died, or were injured. The Confederacy passed the first **conscription** in American history in April of 1862. The Confederate conscription law made all white men between the ages of eighteen and thirty-five liable to be drafted for three years service in the army. There were ways around it, however. A man could legally hire a substitute, and many did. One key exception was that one white man on every plantation with at least twenty enslaved people was exempt. The complaints were so loud, that the law made this war to defend slavery "a rich man's war, but a poor man's fight." Even with the law, the South was desperately short of soldiers by the end of the war. They simply did not have a large enough population to compete with the North in manpower.

The North also passed a conscription law in 1863, when the number of volunteers fell due to defeats and reports of the horrible battles. The Northern law also allowed a person to hire a substitute or escape service by the payment of a $300 fee. That was a huge amount for a

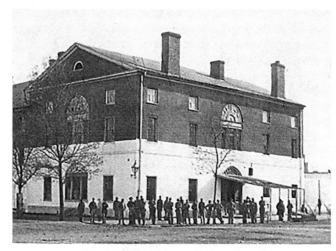

| Old Capital Prison, Washington D.C.

working man, and only the well-to-do could afford that escape. However, the Union army was mainly filled by volunteers who collected bonuses for signing, which they would not get if they were drafted. However, the draft was unpopular and sparked a riot in New York City in July of 1863. The disorder raged for almost a week and was finally suppressed by Union troops called in from the Army of the Potomac.

Another problem experienced by both armies was what to do with prisoners. It had been the long-standing military tradition to parole prisoners on the condition that they would not fight any more, or to exchange them between the armies. However, the South's refusal to recognize black soldiers as prisoners of war and the realization that the South could not afford to replace its soldiers led the North to stop paroles and exchanges. Both sides then had to house and care for thousands of enemy prisoners. More than 50,000 died in the poorly run prison camps. The worst ones were in the South, where there were few resources to spare for Union prisoners.

The worst of the worst among the prison camps was Andersonville prison in Georgia. It was a log stockade with no housing and the only water supply was a sluggish stream that ran through its center. Food was limited to a little cornmeal each day. There was no medical care of any kind. Thirteen thousand Northern soldiers died at that prison. The survivors were little better than living skeletons. The commander of the camp, Captain Henry Wirz, was executed after the war.

As the long, bloody war dragged on, revivals broke out in the army camps. Men who were facing death chose to face God first. The interest in the things of God grew stronger as the war continued. **Chaplains** became common in the army, for they had been rare in previous wars. *Christian History* estimates that a total of between 200,000 and 300,000 soldiers from the two sides accepted Christ as their Savior during the war. (Vol. XI, No. 1, page 30). Leading the list

of committed Christians who served on both sides were Generals Robert E. Lee and Stonewall Jackson.

Chickamauga and Chattanooga. Chattanooga in southeast Tennessee was a key Confederate city after Vicksburg was besieged and captured. The city was an important rail junction that made it the western door to the Confederacy. Confederate General Braxton Bragg, who had met William Rosencrans at the Battle of Murfreesboro, had withdrawn to Chattanooga to set up defenses. All the while, Rosencrans refused to move for months after the battle. In August of 1863, the Union army finally began to move on Chattanooga.

Bragg was not in the same class with Lee and Jackson. He was unsure of himself and acted with excessive caution. The Union army swung around the city, and Bragg became concerned for his supply lines to Atlanta. In early September, Bragg evacuated Chattanooga without firing a single shot in its defense. Rosencrans followed without pausing to rest his army, and the two armies met near Chickamauga Creek on September 19th and 20th.

| Robert E. Lee and "Stonewall" Jackson

| Ulysses S. Grant and William Tecumseh Sherman

Bragg received reinforcements just before the battle. General James Longstreet from Lee's Army of Northern Virginia arrived with two **divisions**. The Confederates broke the Union right flank on the second day of the battle. That part of the army fled the field in wild disarray. A complete collapse was prevented by General George Thomas who held his Union army on the left flank despite everything. His spirited defense allowed the Union army to escape to Chattanooga and earned him the nickname "the Rock of Chickamauga."

Chickamauga was to be the last major Confederate victory. Bragg failed to follow it up. He and his army took up positions in the mountains around the Union army in Chattanooga and began a siege. But unlike the South at Vicksburg, the North had troops it could send to the rescue.

In October of 1863, Ulysses S. Grant was made supreme commander of all Union troops in the west. Rosencrans was also replaced by George Thomas. Grant acted promptly to establish a river supply route to the Union army in Chattanooga. He then brought into the city two more

armies under Generals William T. Sherman and Joseph Hooker. When they were in place, Grant attacked the surrounding Confederates on November 24th.

Hooker's men assaulted the tall, heavily-fortified Lookout Mountain; but the enemy troops there were in bad shape and quickly fell to the Union under the cover of low-lying clouds. When the clouds lifted late in the day, the Stars and Stripes were flying at the top. The newspapers dubbed it the "battle above the clouds."

Sherman attacked the Confederate right flank with little success on the first day. On the second day, Thomas' men were sent to attack some rifle pits in the center of the Confederate line. The men, with pride still wounded from their embarrassing defeat at Chickamauga, took not only the pits but (without orders) drove straight up into the Confederate lines. Thomas' army broke through the rebel defenses at their strongest point and forced them to retreat. Combined with September's capture of Knoxville by General Burnside, the Battle of Chattanooga gave the Union control of Tennessee and an upper hand in the west.

Complete these sentences.

2.56 The Union commander at Chickamauga was _____ and
the Confederate commander was _____ .

2.57 The first conscription law in U.S. history was passed by the _____
government in 1862.

2.58 An estimated _____ to _____ soldiers
became Christians during the war.

2.59 The center of the Confederate line at Chattanooga was overrun by men under the command
of _____ .

2.60 The worst of the Civil War prison camps was _____ in Georgia.

2.61 Northern women established the United States _____
which helped the Union army stay cleaner and healthier.

2.62 A Northern man could avoid the draft by _____ or
_____ .

2.63 The _____ army was better supplied throughout the war.

2.64 _____ was the last major Confederate victory.

2.65 George Thomas earned the nickname "the _____ Chickamauga"
by his stand when the rest of the Union army was fleeing.

2.66 The fighting on Lookout Mountain on November 24th was called the _____
_____ .

2.67 _____ became the supreme Union commander in the
west in October of 1863.

2.68 The standard treatment for any severe injury to a leg or arm was _____ .

2.69 A riot in New York City in July of 1863 was sparked by _____ .

2.70 _____ was a key railroad junction that Bragg evacuated
without firing a shot.

Wilderness to Ford's Theater (1864-65)

Wilderness. Lincoln believed that he had finally found the man he needed to defeat Lee. In March of 1864, Ulysses S. Grant was promoted to the rank of lieutenant general (the first man since George Washington to hold that rank) and given command of all Union forces. He was faced with the task of destroying two major Confederate armies, one in Tennessee now under Joseph Johnston, and the Army of Northern Virginia under Lee. Grant assigned Sherman to command the Union army in Tennessee and advance on Atlanta, Georgia. Grant himself went to the front with the Army of the Potomac that would have to face Robert E. Lee.

The Army of the Potomac marched into Virginia yet again in May of 1864. They came through a heavily wooded area called the Wilderness. Lee attacked there, in an area where the superior Union numbers could not be used effectively because of dense brush, poor visibility, and rough ground. The battle was a mass of confusion. The Union lost about 17,000 men in two days of fighting, and neither side could claim victory. The major difference between Grant and previous commanders was what happened after the battle. Instead of retreating, as every other commander had before him, Grant kept going.

Grant-Lee Duel. Grant shifted his army left and tried to go around Lee. Lee shifted skillfully and met him at Spotsylvania Court House. Again there were huge losses on both sides and victory for neither. Grant could replace his losses, but Lee could not, and Grant knew it. He continued to shift left, forcing Lee to move to meet him, and fighting battles almost daily. Grant was quite content with this strategy and was determined to "fight it out on this line if it takes all summer." It would and then some.

Cold Harbor. As Lee continued to move and block his advance on Richmond, Grant began to lose patience. When the Confederates set up new defensive lines at a town called Cold Harbor, Grant decided to make a strong frontal attack instead of maneuvering again. He sent about a dozen assaults at the Confederate lines, all of which were failures. The Union army suffered over 7,000 casualties in a half an hour. The Confederate lines held.

The slow progress and massive casualties attracted horror in the North. "Butcher Grant" was condemned for his lack of concern for human life, but Grant paid no attention. He had a job to do, and he would keep at it until it was done.

Siege of Petersburg. Grant decided to move yet again in mid-June. This time, he shifted his army south across the James River and marched on the town of Petersburg. Petersburg was a rail junction near Richmond. Most of the trains coming into the Confederate capital came by this route. If Grant captured it, the capital would be at his mercy; however, Lee had time to set up defenses and repulse the Union attack. Grant settled in for a siege.

Atlanta. While Grant was busy in Virginia, William Tecumseh Sherman moved south toward Atlanta, Georgia from Chattanooga. He was opposed by Joseph Johnston's Confederate army. The two sides practiced classic military maneuvering as Sherman worked his way closer and closer to Atlanta from May to July. Johnston's strategy was delay. He fought small battles and withdrew, never allowing Sherman the chance he wanted to destroy the Confederate army. By July Johnston had withdrawn to the strong defenses around Atlanta.

Johnston's strategy was not popular with the Confederate government who wanted Sherman stopped. The Confederate command wanted a more aggressive general, so Johnston was replaced in July by John Bell Hood. Hood attacked Sherman immediately and repeatedly. All the attacks failed and cost the Confederate army irreplaceable soldiers.

In August, Sherman began to shell the city. Morale among the soldiers and citizens fell as the capture of Atlanta seemed imminent. At the end of August, Sherman worked his way around the city and cut off the last railroad link to the Confederacy. Without his supply lines, Hood evacuated the city. Sherman occupied it on August 2nd.

Shenandoah Valley. When Grant settled in to besiege Petersburg, another Union army under David Hunter was working its way down the key Shenandoah Valley. The valley ran northeast in Virginia toward Washington D.C. It was a rich, fertile area that supplied the Confederate army with food. The Union had been unable to gain control of it thus far in the war.

Lee sent Jubal Early to the valley. He was able to stop Hunter and even threatened Washington for a short time. Grant was determined to end this threat that distracted him from concentrating on Lee. He sent Philip Sheridan in with express orders to clear the valley so clean of everything that "a crow could not cross it without carrying its own food." Early succeeded in surprising Sheridan's men at Cedar Creek on October 19th. The Confederates were forced back and were not able to challenge the Union after that. Sheridan proceeded to obey his orders, burning crops and buildings, driving off livestock, and depriving the Confederacy of anything of value in the valley. Using these methods, the Union finally took control of the valley.

This was total war. Prior to the Civil War, American armies avoided harming farms, industries, or any non-military target. But Grant, Sherman, and Sheridan realized that the farms and industries kept the army going. The destruction brought the war home to the ordinary people whose support was vital if the war was to continue. The Union began a new policy to destroy anything that might aid the Confederate army in the hope it would force the civilian population to sue for peace.

| David Farragut and his crew

Mobile. The port of Mobile, Alabama was a major port for blockade runners during the war. By mid-1864, it was also one of the few Confederate ports still open. The city's defenses included three forts, four gunboats (including one ironclad), underwater obstacles, and mines (called torpedoes). Admiral David Farragut, the commander who captured New Orleans, had organized a fleet to take the city. They attacked on August 5, 1864.

One of the Union ironclads was blown up by a torpedo early in the attack. When the other ships hesitated, Farragut gave the famous order, "Damn the torpedoes! Full speed ahead!" The fleet got past the outer defenses and into the harbor. The engines on the Confederate ironclad failed, and the forts were pounded into submission. The port was captured on August 23rd, but the city itself would not surrender for months.

| Civil War-era Navy

Election of 1864. The elections came around in 1864 with Lincoln running for a second term as president. The American democracy was still the only major one in the world and very much a unique experiment. It was astonishing that in the midst of Civil War carnage a regular election could even be held; but it proceeded in an orderly fashion, displaying the incredible strength and flexibility of the American republic.

The war was unpopular, having dragged on far longer than anyone dreamed it should have. A group of Northern Democrats called the Copperheads violently opposed the war, some to the point of treason. Other "War Democrats" supported the war and the Republican president. These joined with the Republicans in 1864 to form the temporary National Union Party and nominate Lincoln for president. One of the War Democrats named Andrew Johnson was nominated as his vice-president.

The remaining Democrats nominated George McClellan, the army general dismissed for his hesitancy in battle. Their platform was defeatist, calling the war a failure. McClellan, as a soldier who had fought in the war, disavowed the plank, but he would have been under immense pressure to negotiate an end to the war had he won. The Democrats had a chance as long as the war was going badly, but the victories at Atlanta, Mobile, and the Shenandoah Valley revived the Republican cause. Many Americans agreed with Lincoln's slogan "Don't swap horses in the middle of the river." Lincoln won easily and that ended the Confederacy's last realistic hope. The war would continue.

Name the person, event, battle, or item.

2.71 _____ rail junction near Richmond, besieged by Grant beginning June 1864

2.72 _____ man Lee sent to Shenandoah Valley to confront Hunter

2.73 _____ Grant lost 7,000 men in a half an hour in a vain attack on Confederate lines

2.74 _____ the dense trees kept Grant from using his superior numbers against Lee

2.75 _____ man who said "Damn the torpedoes! Full speed ahead!"

2.76 _____ Democratic nominee for president 1864

2.77 _____ Lincoln's running mate in 1864

2.78 _____ Union commander that captured Atlanta

2.79 _____ the name of the anti-war Northern Democrats

2.80 _____ Union man who laid waste to the Shenandoah Valley

2.81 _____ Confederate port captured August 23, 1864

2.82 _____ group of Democrats that joined with the Republicans in 1864

2.83 _____ commander who replaced Johnston in the west and immediately attacked Sherman

2.84 _____ rank given to Grant when he took command of all Union troops

Answer these questions.

2.85 How was Grant different from all previous Union commanders?

_____

_____

2.86 What event ended the Confederacy's last hope?

_____

2.87 What was Grant's strategy to defeat Lee?

_____

_____

2.88 What is total war?

_____

_____

Nashville. General Hood still had a Confederate army around Atlanta after Sherman captured the city. He unsuccessfully tried to cut Sherman's supply lines and force him to retreat. After several attempts through the fall, Hood decided on a desperate strategy. He would march north toward the Union-held city of Nashville. He hoped to force Sherman to abandon Atlanta and pursue him.

However, Sherman had other plans. He kept his army in Georgia and sent George Thomas, the "Rock of Chickamauga," north to take over the defense of Nashville. Thomas built up an army in the city as Hood worked his way north, pressing a small Union force that was fighting a delaying retreat in front of him. Hood reached Nashville in early December. By that time, Thomas had built up an army that was larger than his Confederate attackers.

Hood lacked the men to overrun the heavy defenses at Nashville. He also did not have enough men to effectively besiege it. He could not go around it without risking an attack by Thomas' forces. Out of all options except retreat, he stayed until Thomas was ready to attack.

On December 15th and 16th, the Union army attacked and destroyed Hood's army. The scattered remains fled south. What was left was no longer a threat to the Union.

Sherman's March to the Sea. William Tecumseh Sherman realized that with Hood's army to the north there was no one in the Confederacy that could stop him. He therefore proposed to take the war into the heart of the rebel states and make Georgia howl. Grant and Lincoln gave him permission to march from Atlanta to the sea, living off the land and destroying everything of value in his path. He destroyed much of Atlanta and marched out on November 15, 1864. During the march he had no communication with the North. He literally disappeared for a month.

Sherman's march to the sea was devastating to Georgia and the South. It aroused bitter hatred and fear. It showed that the Confederate armies could no longer protect their people. Buildings, railroads, farms, crops, and homes were systematically destroyed all along Sherman's route. Sherman's army ate well on captured food and had enough left over to supply the horde of escaping slaves that joined them along the route. Sherman reached the coast and contacted the blockade fleet on December 10th. Resupplied by the fleet, he captured Savannah on December 21st.

After Savannah, Sherman and his men headed north into South Carolina. That state had been the leader in the secession. The Union army was particularly vicious there. The capital of Columbia was burned on February 17th. Sherman cut the railroad lines into Charleston, forcing that city to surrender to the Union forces that were besieging it. Shortly after that, a combined force from the army and navy captured Wilmington, N.C. which was the last open Confederate port. Meanwhile, Sherman marched into North Carolina. The remaining Confederate army under the command of Joseph Johnston did not have the strength to even slow him down.

Petersburg. While Sheridan and Sherman had been moving, Grant had been in place at Petersburg. All through the end of 1864 and the first part of 1865, he had kept up the pressure on the Confederate defenses. Grant had tried several unsuccessful assaults with devastating losses; however, the fighting, disease, and desertions had steadily reduced the Confederate army. They were now desperately short of basic supplies and were hungry. Grant had slowly spread his lines west, forcing Lee to spread his own limited army out further and further. Grant hoped to eventually outflank Lee (move around the side of his army) and fight a decisive battle.

Lee decided to attempt an attack before the Union succeeded in encircling his army. The Confederate attack on March 25th successfully captured Fort Stedman, a focal point on the Union lines. Lee hoped to use it to threaten Grant's supply lines, but the Union counter-attacked and recaptured the fort the same day.

Meanwhile, Philip Sheridan had finished the Shenandoah Valley and rejoined the Union army at Petersburg. Grant now sent him

| Appomattox Court House, where the Confederate Army surrendered

around Lee's lines to the west to attack Five Forks which controlled Lee's last remaining supply line. The attack on April 1st was successful. Grant ordered a general attack all along the Union lines. The Confederate defenders were spread too thin, and their lines broke. Lee ordered a retreat and informed Jefferson Davis that he could no longer protect Richmond.

Appomattox Court House. After the fall of Petersburg, the Confederate government abandoned Richmond and fled south. Lee also headed south, hoping to join up with Johnston's forces in South Carolina. Grant followed in close pursuit. In the meantime, Sheridan got between Lee and Johnston, forcing the former to turn west. Things went from bad to worse for the Confederate army when food rations failed to arrive. At Sayler's Creek, the Union army attacked the retreating Confederates, capturing their supply wagons and thousands of prisoners. Finally, Lee realized he had no choice "but to go and see General Grant." He then added, "I would rather die a thousand deaths."

Lee and Grant met on April 9th in a small settlement called Appomattox Court House. Lee chose to surrender rather than disband his army and continue fighting a guerrilla war that would drive the nation into further barbarism and bloodshed. Grant returned the favor by granting the Army of Northern Virginia full parole if they laid down their arms. This meant that Lee and the other Confederate leaders would not be hanged as traitors. Grant even allowed the soldiers to keep their horses and sent rations over to the hungry Confederate army. The Army of Northern Virginia formally surrendered on April 12, 1865, four years to the day after Fort Sumter.

For all practical purposes, the war was over. Joseph Johnston realized he had no hope of continuing alone. On April 26th, he surrendered to Sherman on the same terms given to General Lee. Jefferson Davis was captured by Union cavalry on May 10th in Georgia. The last battle of the war was fought three days later near Brownsville, Texas. Federal troops arrived in Galveston, Texas on June 19,1865 to take control of the state and ensure that all enslaved people be freed. Juneteenth (short for "June Nineteenth") marks the day. Juneteenth honors the end to slavery in the United States and is considered the longest-running African American holiday.

Conclusions. The Civil War cost the United States over 600,000 men. Slavery was ended, and the notion that a state could leave the Union was abandoned. The United States was again one nation, and its government was stronger than ever before. Union industry had grown stronger under the demands of a war economy. The South, on the other hand, was devastated. Four million black Americans were no longer slaves, but they had no jobs and no education. Victory brought both great gain and great pain.

Ford's Theatre. The last wound that convulsed the nation was the assassination of Abraham Lincoln. Lincoln had held the Union together and pressed forward with the war. He had managed the infighting in his cabinet, opponents in Congress, poor generals, bad luck, and disappointment with skill and courage for four years. After Appomattox, the president decided to relax. He and his wife went to Ford's Theatre on April 14, 1865 to see a comedy. There, he was shot in the back of the head by a deranged actor named John Wilkes Booth, who thought he was avenging the South. Lincoln was carried across the street and died early on April 15th.

Booth fled from the scene. He was tracked by federal troops and shot after being cornered in a barn. Several people who had conspired with him to kill other members of the U.S. government were hanged. Lincoln's body was taken back to Springfield, Illinois in a slow-moving train for burial. His death coming so close on the heels of victory plunged the nation into grief and inspired a cry for revenge that echoed ominously through the South.

| John Wilkes Booth's Wanted Poster

Answer true or false.

If the answer is false, change it to make it true. Merely adding the word "not" is not sufficient.

2.89 _____ Sherman marched from Nashville to the sea, destroying anything of military value in his path.

2.90 _____ The Confederate army in Tennessee was virtually destroyed outside of Nashville in December 1864.

2.91 _____ Lee retreated from Petersburg in January of 1865.

2.92 _____ Over six hundred thousand men died in the Civil War.

2.93 _____ Lincoln was assassinated by John Wilkes Booth.

2.94 _____ Lee surrendered at Richmond in April, 1865.

2.95 _____ Grant led the troops that captured Five Forks.

2.96 _____ George Thomas was the Union victor at Nashville.

2.97 _____ Sherman captured Savannah in December 1864.

2.98 _____ The Confederate government was captured when Richmond fell.

2.99 _____ The surrender of Lee ended the war for all practical purposes.

2.100 _____ Lincoln's assassination occurred at Ford's Theater on April 14, 1865.

2.101 _____ Grant allowed the Confederate soldiers to keep their rifles after they surrendered.

2.102 _____ Booth was hanged after a trial.

2.103 _____ By the end, the Confederate army at Petersburg was hungry and short of basic supplies.

2.104 _____ Meade forced Lee to spread his defensive lines further and further at Petersburg.

Write a one-page paper.

2.105 Write a paper on the Emancipation Proclamation, a Civil War battle, a general, weapons used in the war, or the living conditions of the soldiers.

TEACHER CHECK _____ _____
                              initials   date

↺ **Review the material in this section in preparation for the Self Test.** This Self Test will check your mastery of this particular section as well as your knowledge of the previous section.

SELF TEST 2

Match the correct person. Some answers will be used more than once (each answer, 2 points).

2.01	_____ devastated the Shenandoah Valley	a. Robert E. Lee
2.02	_____ led the Union army at Gettysburg	b. Ulysses S. Grant
2.03	_____ president of the Confederacy	c. George McClellan
2.04	_____ led the Confederate army at Gettysburg	d. Stonewall Jackson
2.05	_____ the "Rock of Chickamauga"	e. William T. Sherman
2.06	_____ dismissed from Union command for being repeatedly hesitant	f. David Farragut
		g. John Brown
2.07	_____ Gettysburg Address	h. George Meade
2.08	_____ first U.S. lieutenant general since Washington	i. Jefferson Davis
		j. Abraham Lincoln
2.09	_____ Union commander who defeated Hood at Nashville	k. George Thomas
2.010	_____ captured Vicksburg	l. Joseph Johnston
2.011	_____ Lee's brilliant subordinate, shot by friendly fire at Chancellorsville	m. Philip Sheridan
2.012	_____ captured New Orleans and Mobile	
2.013	_____ delayed Sherman on his way to Atlanta, relieved of command for not being aggressive	
2.014	_____ abolitionist martyr, attacked Harpers Ferry to start slave uprising	
2.015	_____ devastated Georgia in a march to the sea	

Put a *U* beside the Union victories and a *C* beside the Confederate victories (each answer, 1 point).

In cases where a victor was not clear, choose the side that benefited most from the results of the battle.

2.016 _____ Chancellorsville

2.017 _____ Gettysburg

2.018 _____ Antietam

2.019 _____ First Bull Run

2.020 _____ Peninsular Campaign

2.021 _____ *Monitor* and *Merrimac*

2.022 _____ Shiloh

2.023 _____ Chickamauga

2.024 _____ Petersburg

2.025 _____ Fredericksburg

Name the person, event, or term (each answer, 2 points).

2.026 _____ Act that ended the era of compromise

2.027 _____ Supreme Court decision that protected slavery in all the states

2.028 _____ document that freed the slaves in all states still in rebellion on January 1, 1863

2.029 _____ battle that was the turning point of the Civil War

2.030 _____ man who was the outgoing U.S. president when the Confederate states were first organized

2.031 _____ the worst prison camp in the Civil War

2.032 _____ killed more soldiers than bullets did during the Civil War

2.033 _____ place where Robert E. Lee surrendered

2.034 _____ man who killed Abraham Lincoln

2.035 _____ first state to secede from the Union

Answer these questions (each answer, 3 points).

2.036 What were two advantages the South had in the Civil War?

a. _____

b. _____

2.037 How was Grant different from all previous Union commanders?

_____

_____

2.038 What were two reasons why Britain did not support the Confederacy?

a. _____

b. _____

2.039 What was the political stand of the Republican Party and Abraham Lincoln on slavery in the election of 1860?

_____

_____

2.040 Why was the Kansas Territory called "Bleeding Kansas?"

_____

_____

2.041 Which army had the advantage in the area of supplies and why?

_____

_____

2.042 What was remarkable about the election of 1864?

_____

_____

2.043 Why were there so many battle casualties in the Civil War?

_____

_____

Answer true or false (each answer, 1 point).

2.044 _____ Soldiers in both armies became more interested in God as the war continued.

2.045 _____ More Americans died in the Civil War than in any other war fought by the U.S.

2.046 _____ The fall of Vicksburg gave the Union control of the Ohio River.

2.047 _____ Missouri was a slave state that stayed in the Union.

2.048 _____ Ulysses S. Grant is considered by most experts to have been the best general in the Civil War.

2.049 _____ The first Southern states seceded directly after the election of Abraham Lincoln.

2.050 _____ The Union government passed America's first conscription law.

2.051 _____ Black soldiers were quickly incorporated with white soldiers on equal terms in the Union army.

2.052 _____ Both sides expected a long, hard war from the beginning.

2.053 _____ Lincoln came to national attention through his work as secretary of state.

| 80 / 100 | SCORE _____ | TEACHER _____ _____ |
| | | initials   date |

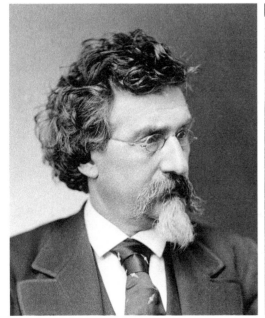 

| Mathew Brady, the most famous photographer of the Civil War.

3. RECONSTRUCTION

The nation faced many problems at the end of the Civil War. The victorious Union had to decide how much to punish the South for secession. The South had to form new state governments acceptable to the North. The rights of the newly freed black Americans needed to be defined, and those rights had to be protected. Moreover, the South itself was in ruins and lacked the funds needed to rebuild.

Many of the people in the North called for harsh treatment of the former Confederate States. However, Abraham Lincoln was not among them. In his second Inaugural Address about a month before his death, Lincoln spoke of his own goals in the victory which was quickly approaching.

> With malice toward none, with charity for all, with firmness in the right as God gives us to see the right, let us strive on to finish the work we are in, to bind up the nation's wounds, to care for him who shall have borne the battle and for his widow and orphan, to do all which may achieve and cherish a just and lasting peace among ourselves and with all nations.

Unfortunately for the South, Lincoln did not survive to pursue his peace. The new president, Andrew Johnson, did not have Lincoln's flexibility or political skill. After he butted heads with Congress, the Radical Republicans in that body set up their own harsh "Reconstruction" of the South over the president's vetoes. They even **impeached** Johnson for opposing them.

The Southern states all had acceptable state governments by 1870. By 1877 all of those states had white Democrats in complete control. That same year, newly elected President Rutherford B. Hayes moved out the last federal troops in the South that were supporting occupation governments. That was the final end of the long ordeal known as Reconstruction.

SECTION OBJECTIVES

Review these objectives. When you have completed this section, you should be able to:

6. Describe Reconstruction.
7. Describe the background and policies of Civil War-era presidents.
8. Describe the post-Civil War corruption.
9. Explain the status of black Americans during and after Reconstruction.

VOCABULARY

Study these words to enhance your learning success in this section.

alderman (äl' der man). Member of a city legislature.

filibuster (fil' a bus ter). In the U.S. Senate, a senator or group of senators refuse to stop debating a bill and thus prevent it from passing.

impeach (im pēch'). To charge a public official with misconduct in office in front of the proper authority for a trial.

posthumous (päs chu mus). Born after the death of the father.

Presidential Reconstruction

Andrew Johnson (1808-1875). Andrew Johnson was the first U.S. president to be impeached by Congress. Johnson was born to poor working parents in North Carolina. His father died when he was three. He had no formal education. At the age of thirteen, he was apprenticed to a tailor, which is probably when he learned to read.

As a youth, Johnson worked his way to Tennessee where he set up a successful tailoring business. He married the daughter of a shoemaker. She taught him to write, do simple arithmetic, and encouraged him to read. Johnson's business prospered, and he purchased property (including slaves) in Tennessee.

As Johnson's social position improved, he went into politics as a Jacksonian Democrat. He developed a powerful voice and used it to influence crowds. He won his first election in 1829 as an **alderman**, and he rarely lost after that. He served as a mayor, state representative, state senator, and governor in Tennessee. He served as a member of both the U.S. House and Senate.

Andrew Johnson believed in the right of Southerners to own enslaved people, but was an even stronger supporter of the Union. He was a member of the U.S. Senate in 1860 and was the only Southern senator who refused to secede with his state. Lincoln appointed him as military governor of his home state of Tennessee as it was conquered by the Union. As a prominent member of the War Democrats who supported Lincoln throughout the Civil War, he was an obvious choice for vice president in 1864. He filled out the ticket of the National Union Party which combined the Republicans and War Democrats to nominate Lincoln in 1864. He became president when Lincoln died.

Johnson's Reconstruction Plan. In 1863 Lincoln had established a plan to readmit the Confederate States to the Union. It was called the 10 percent plan. It required that only 10 percent of the voters in a state take an oath of loyalty to the Union. These would elect a state government that accepted the abolition of slavery. Then the state would be readmitted to the Union with all rights and privileges. Several conquered Confederate states had complied with these terms and sent representatives to Congress by 1864.

Congress refused to allow the new Congressmen to take their seats. (Congress has this right under the Constitution). Many in Congress felt that Lincoln's plan was too lenient. They hoped that Johnson, who hated rich planters because of his own humble background, would take a harder line with the South.

However, Johnson was a Southern Democrat and a follower of Andrew Jackson (a believer in restricted government). He set up a Reconstruction program in 1865 based on Lincoln's plans. Once 10% of voters had taken a loyalty oath, they were to vote for members of a special state convention. The convention had to approve the Thirteenth Amendment (which ended slavery), repudiate Confederate debts, and repeal the state's secession from Union. Certain high-level Confederates and those owning more than $20,000 in property were required to get a presidential pardon to vote, but Johnson granted those freely.

The Southern states quickly complied with these easy terms. The new state governments moved with equal swiftness in passing "Black Codes" that insured the black population would continue to be a subjugated people. The codes varied from state to state, but they basically worked to keep blacks as a cheap labor supply for the South. Black workers had to sign labor contracts with their employers. They lost all of their pay or could be dragged back by force if they tried to leave before the contract was finished. They could not vote, serve on juries, and in many states they could not own or lease land. Some states even declared that black people without jobs could be arrested for "idleness." They would be forced to work to pay their fines or serve on chain gangs rented out by the government. Everything possible was done to insure that the only change in the South was that black people were no longer *technically* slaves.

Abolitionists in the North were furious at the blatant defiance to the goals of the Union. To make matters worse, many of newly elected Southern Congressmen had been high-ranking Confederates, including Alexander Stephens, the Confederate vice president! The Republicans had enjoyed complete control of Congress during the war years. Several pro-Northern laws had passed during those four years, including a Homestead Act (giving free land to settlers), a high tariff, and subsidies for a Northern railroad across the nation. Northern Republicans were not anxious to surrender power, especially on such easy terms.

Johnson vs. Congress. An angry Congress now challenged Johnson's easy terms for the South. They were led by Thaddeus Stevens, a representative with a long history of championing the cause of black Americans. He led a group called the "Radical Republicans," Congressmen who pushed for a harsh policy toward the South. They were especially concerned with securing the rights of the newly freed black people, hoping to secure them as Republican voters.

Under the leadership of Stevens, Congress again refused to give the former Confederate states their seats in the national legislature. Then Congress formed the Joint (House-Senate) Committee on Reconstruction. Stevens, as chairman of the House members, quickly became the strongest influence on the committee. Stevens used his position to pursue plans that offered more protection to the newly freed slaves and less power to their defeated masters.

At first, Congress simply tried to modify the Johnson-Lincoln Plan to include more protection for the freedmen. In February of 1866,

| Andrew Johnson and a group of freedmen

Congress passed a law extending the life of the Freedmen's Bureau. The Freedmen's Bureau was a organization created to aid black people in their change from slaves to citizens. It operated as an early welfare agency, distributing clothes and food, providing education, settling disputes with employers, and hopefully settling the newly freed men on their own small farms. Southerners resented the Bureau, especially in its attempts to educate black people. Johnson vetoed the law to continue the Bureau because it interfered with the rights of the Southern states.

The now very angry Congress passed the Civil Rights Act which gave black people the rights of citizenship and tried to offset some of the Black Codes. Johnson vetoed that law as well, but in April Congress overrode the veto, making the bill a law. It was the first time Congress had ever successfully overridden a presidential veto on a piece of major legislation. It would be the first of many for President Johnson.

Congress wanted to insure that a future Democratic Congress could not undo the Civil Rights Act, so they passed the Fourteenth Amendment to the Constitution and sent it to the states. The Amendment made all freedmen citizens. It also ended the representation in Congress of any state that did not allow them to vote. However, it did not *require* that states allow black people to vote. Even many Northern states did not allow that. The Amendment barred certain Confederates from office and voided Confederate debts.

Johnson opposed the Fourteenth Amendment, but he had no power to prevent it. The loss of Lincoln was keenly felt as the relationship between the president and Congress deteriorated. Lincoln, the flexible political genius, would have understood the need to compromise with and then lead Congress, but Johnson was simply defiant. He went on a speaking tour in the summer of 1866, trying to influence the congressional elections. He hoped to get a Congress that favored his Reconstruction plan. Instead, his "swing around the circle" gained votes for the radicals. Johnson's fiery speeches were mercilessly heckled and rapidly became shouting matches between the president and the crowd. In the end, the 1866 elections expanded the number of Radical Republicans in Washington.

Johnson compounded his problems by failing to recognize dangerous reality. He encouraged the Southern states to reject the Fourteenth Amendment. Tennessee was the only one of the former Confederate states to vote in favor of the amendment. Congress now had solid, veto-proof majorities in both houses, and decided to set up its own Reconstruction plan when it met in 1867.

 Answer these questions.

3.1 Under Johnson and Lincoln's plan, what percent of Southern voters had to take a loyalty oath to begin rebuilding the state government? _____

3.2 What did the state conventions have to do before they could reform as a government under Johnson's plan?

a. _____

b. _____

c. _____

3.3   What were the Republican Congressmen who favored harsh treatment of the South called?

_____

3.4   What Amendment to the Constitution ended slavery? _____

3.5   What was Andrew Johnson's trade? _____

3.6   What law did Congress pass to offset the Black Codes?

_____

3.7   What organization tried to aid the black people in the transition to freedom?

_____

3.8   How did Congress react to Johnson's veto of the Civil Rights Bill?

_____

3.9   What were the terms of the Fourteenth Amendment?

a.   _____

b.   _____

c.   _____

d.   _____

3.10   Why did Johnson make his "swing around the circle?"

_____

_____

3.11   Why did Johnson veto the extension of the Freedman's Bureau?

_____

3.12   What laws had the Republican Congress passed when the Democratic South was in rebellion?

a.   _____

b.   _____

c.   _____

3.13   What was the purpose of the "Black Codes?"

_____

_____

3.14   Which former Confederate state did accept the Fourteenth Amendment before 1867?

_____

3.15   What party nominated Johnson for vice president in 1864?

_____

3.16 What was unusual about Andrew Johnson as a senator in 1860?

_____

3.17 What Congressional committee tried to change Johnson's Reconstruction plan?

_____

3.18 Who was the leader of the Radical Republicans? _____

Radical Reconstruction

Occupation. Beginning in March of 1867, Congress began to model Reconstruction according to its own ideas, overriding every presidential veto. With the exception of Tennessee, the South was divided into five military districts run by a general and controlled by federal troops. The state governments were placed under military control, and former Confederate leaders were denied the right to vote. The states were required to ratify the Fourteenth Amendment and guarantee the right of black people to vote before they were allowed to form a new government. Moreover, another law was passed that required all of Johnson's orders to the army be issued through Ulysses S. Grant, whom the Republicans felt could be trusted to interpret them as Congress wished.

Southern reaction to the new laws was bitterly hostile. Not only were their own white leaders denied the right to even vote, black people would be voting! They were especially bitter at the hypocrisy that some Northern states still denied black people the right to vote. The rapid registration of black voters and the fact these new citizens voted Republican enforced Southern fears of a political conspiracy to take over the South. But by 1870, all of the states had new governments and constitutions that met Congressional criteria.

As a result of the new laws, Republican governments came to power in most of the states. Most of them also had a minority of black representatives, which inflamed the bigoted South. (Only in South Carolina did black representatives constitute a majority in the state assembly.) A few black Americans were also elected to the U.S. House and Senate. The Radical Republicans tried to protect these gains by passing the Fifteenth Amendment which guaranteed freedmen the right to vote. It was ratified in 1870.

Impeachment. Congress was so successful in pushing its own agenda that it began to reach for more power by getting rid of their main annoyance, the president. They tried to do this by passing the Tenure of Office Act (over Johnson's veto). This law supposedly forbade the president to fire any official approved by the Senate without the approval of that same body. This meant Johnson could not legally dismiss members of his own cabinet, his own personal advisors!

As expected, Johnson violated the law in 1868 when he dismissed Secretary of War Edwin Stanton who was a Radical supporter. Congress immediately voted to impeach Johnson for "high crimes and misdemeanors" as required by the Constitution. Most of the charges stemmed from firing Stanton, although he was also accused of verbal assaults on Congress.

The impeachment trial in the Senate was a huge show. The House prosecuted the case badly. Johnson's skillful attorneys showed that Johnson's only crime was opposing Congress. Still the Radical control of the Senate meant the vote would be close, and in the end Johnson was acquitted by a single vote. Seven Republican senators had voted in his favor, defying their own party for the sake of justice. Johnson had been stubborn and impolitic, but the Senate jury decided he had not committed a crime. The vote saved the presidency from a dangerous precedent. Impeachment could not be used as a political tool to remove an unpopular president.

Carpetbaggers and Scalawags. In the meantime, Reconstruction governments came to be dominated by Northerners who had traveled south and Southerners who decided to cooperate with Reconstruction. The former were called "carpetbaggers," because they supposedly traveled south with their possessions in a carpetbag to get rich yielding political power in the South. The latter group were called "scalawags" and were considered traitors to the Southern cause.

Some of the carpetbaggers did get rich by using their elected offices for personal gain. Others came south because they saw the Southern country while serving in the war and wanted to settle there. Still others came to bring Northern justice and ideas to the "backward" South. They were extremely unpopular, and stealing done by a prominent few of them reflected badly on the entire group.

The scalawags also had mixed reasons for cooperating. Many felt that they had lost the war and that cooperation was the proper course of action. Others saw the Republican Party as the only chance to put white people back in power. Still others were just switching sides to make a quick buck.

The corruption in the Reconstruction governments mirrored corruption in the entire nation. It varied, depending on the honesty of the men in power, but it also attracted a great deal of attention. As the years passed, Northerners saw the corruption as a reason to end Reconstruction. They eventually became tired of trying to control the South and believed that *white* Southerners should control their democratic governments.

| Sharecropper

Reconstruction governments did do some good. They instituted badly needed reforms in Southern governments. Public schools were established, tax systems were modernized, and internal improvements had begun. But the leaders of the old South would not tolerate being dominated by Northerners who promoted equality. The deep racial hatred of the Southern white people controlled their views of government and justice. They eventually found ways to regain power: violence, intimidation, and fraud.

"Redeemers." Some bitter Southern whites resorted to secret associations and terror to regain control of their governments. The Ku Klux Klan, formed in Tennessee in 1866, was the most infamous of these organizations. Dressed in white masks, these men would attack Northern Republicans, male teachers at freedmen schools, and Southerners who cooperated with the Reconstruction governments. But most of their fury was unleashed on black people who dared to exercise their newfound rights.

Black Americans were threatened, beaten, or killed for voting, getting an education, not acting in a subservient manner, or daring to challenge a white man in court.

Using these methods, the Klan and other organizations drove the Republicans out of the South. Only Democratic votes were acceptable, and by 1877, all the Southern states were "redeemed" as white Democrats came back into power. They remained in power for a long time. The deep bitterness of the Reconstruction period kept the Republican Party from having any large following in the South for many years.

Situation in the South. The South settled down to a new form of society. The old aristocratic planter society was gone. The lack of cash after the war meant that landowners had no way to pay laborers to work their fields. This led to the "share crop" system. In exchange for use of the land and tools, a worker (usually black) would raise a crop and split it with the landowner (usually white).

The white storekeepers and landowners charged high prices for tools and supplies. They also paid low prices for crops such as cotton. This led to a type of debt-slavery that kept thousands of black Americans in poverty for generations. High costs drove many of the landowners into debt and forced them to rely on heavily on cotton for needed cash. The concentration on one crop exhausted the soil and made poverty worse.

The Fourteenth Amendment gave black people the rights of citizenship, but equality was carefully evaded. Separate facilities were set up all over the South for eating, traveling, and learning. Tax dollars from the white-controlled legislatures invariably favored white facilities. Black schools received much less money than white schools; that is, until the system was overthrown in the 1960s.

The Fifteenth Amendment, which gave black people the right to vote, was virtually ignored.

Black people who dared to vote faced the threat of violence from the Klan and other white supremacist organizations. Southern governments resorted to fraud and restrictive laws to prevent black Americans from voting. For example, some states required voters to pass literacy tests. White people routinely passed and black people routinely failed. Other states passed "grandfather clauses" that only allowed men to vote if their ancestors had in 1860. Poverty, poor education, and denial of the right to vote kept black Americans from truly being free, even after a devastating war had been fought for just that purpose.

Seward's Folly. By 1867, Andrew Johnson was little more than a figurehead, but his administration did manage one true victory, the purchase of Alaska. That territory was the property of the nation of Russia in the early 1860s. The czar saw the cold land in North America as a liability in the event of war with Britain. So he offered to sell it to the United States, which was another nation often at odds with the English.

Johnson's secretary of state was William Seward, a man who favored expansion, and he willingly negotiated a treaty offering Russia $7.2 million for the land (about two cents an acre). Most of the people in the United States saw no use for a piece of land so far north. It could not be used for farms, which is what most Americans wanted. The popular press called it "Seward's Folly" or "Seward's Icebox." Nevertheless, Congress approved the treaty, and the land has since repaid its purchase price many times over in oil, gold, fish, and minerals.

| William H. Seward, secretary of state 1861-1869

 Complete these sentences.

3.19 Northern men who became part of the Reconstruction governments in the South were called

_____ .

3.20 The South was divided into _____ military districts under Radical Reconstruction.

3.21 The purchase of Alaska was mocked by calling it _____ .

3.22 Many black farmers were put into debt-slavery by the _____ system.

3.23 Southern white people regained control of their governments using terror and secret societies

like the _____ .

3.24 Freedmen were given the right to vote by the _____ Amendment.

3.25 _____ Republicans voted to acquit Johnson at his impeachment.

3.26 The Radical Congress required Johnson to issue all his orders to the army through

_____ .

3.27 The United States paid _____ dollars for Alaska.

3.28 Johnson was impeached for violating the _____ Act.

3.29 Due to bitter feelings over Reconstruction, the South was dominated by the

_____ Party for many years.

3.30 _____ were Southern men who cooperated with Reconstruction.

3.31 A Southern state was "_____" when white Democrats were again in power.

3.32 Johnson was impeached when he fired _____ .

Answer these questions.

3.33 How did the South avoid the Fifteenth Amendment?

a. _____

b. _____

c. _____

3.34 Why did Northern people begin to oppose Reconstruction as time went by?

a. _____

b. _____

c. _____

3.35 How did the Southern Democrats regain control of their governments?

_____

_____

3.36 What good did Reconstruction governments do?

a. _____

b. _____

c. _____

3.37 Why did the South continue to rely on cotton and what did it do to the soil?

a. _____

b. _____

3.38 How did the education system in the South hurt black Americans?

_____

_____

3.39 Why was the outcome of Johnson's impeachment so important?

_____

_____

Era of Good Stealings

Election of 1868. General Ulysses S. Grant slowly turned against Andrew Johnson. By the time Johnson was impeached, Grant was openly siding with the Republicans in Congress. His immense popularity made him an obvious choice for president in 1868. He was nominated by the Republicans along with a platform that called for harsh Reconstruction and repayment of Union Civil War debts. The Democrats nominated New York's Governor Horatio Seymour to oppose him. Their platform denounced Radical Reconstruction and called for debts to be repaid in inflationary paper money, not specie.

The Republican campaign involved a great deal of "waving the bloody shirt" (reminding the public about the war). The Democrats were accused of supporting the rebellion. "Vote as you shot" was a popular Republican slogan. Grant won the election by a comfortable majority. However, many white people in the South could not vote, and the black voters gave Grant the margin of victory. The unpopular Andrew Johnson was not even considered for the Democratic nomination, but he remained active in Tennessee politics. He was again elected to the U.S. Senate in 1875, just prior to his death.

Ulysses S. Grant (1822-1885). Ulysses S. Grant was an honest man who had one of the most corrupt administrations in American history. He was an excellent general, but one of the nation's worst presidents. He was born in Ohio to a tanner. His father had a prosperous business, and the shy Ulysses was given a good education. He became an excellent horseman, but had a distinct lack of business sense and no interest in his father's profession.

His father succeeded in getting him an appointment to West Point in 1839. Grant was an average student who did well in mathematics and horsemanship. He served in the Mexican War and received a promotion for his conduct. After the war, he married a classmate's sister and continued his career in the army.

| Ulysses S. Grant as President

In 1853, he was posted in an isolated fort in California, far from his beloved and growing family. He lost money in several schemes, began drinking, and eventually resigned from the army.

Until the Civil War, he worked at a variety of unsuccessful jobs. When the war began, he helped organize volunteers and was eventually given a colonel's command because the army badly needed experienced officers. He quickly gained fame for his victories in the west and was promoted to command of the entire Union army in 1864. He was the man who finally cornered Robert E. Lee. He was praised, even in the South, for the generous terms he gave to his defeated foe.

Grant was not well suited for the presidency. He was shy, naive, and a poor judge of character.

His own honesty is supported by historians, but he constantly chose men for important offices who were extremely dishonest. He was easily swayed by these men to do what they wanted, and he continued to be loyal to them after their misdeeds were exposed. The result was an out-of-control administration that can be called the "Era of Good Stealings."

The new president was in a mess from the beginning. His cabinet was generally made up of friends without any consideration of their abilities. (Hamilton Fish, his very competent secretary of state, was an exception). The nation was in need of civil service reform to end the system of giving government jobs to pay off political supporters. Grant initially favored reform, but his "friends" talked him out of it. Grant's in-laws especially benefited from the old plan, many of them landing government jobs. Grant also abandoned his initial plans to ease up on Reconstruction after pressure from the party.

Boss Tweed. The necessities of war had created an atmosphere of waste and fraud. Many businessmen had become rich supplying the needs of the army. Graft, corruption, and dishonesty became the dominant features of the get-rich-quick mindset. Cheating the government, investors, buyers, and anyone else became commonplace. Judges, police, and legislators were routinely bribed to look the other way. Millions were made by entrepreneurs who overcharged their own railroads for construction costs, sold stocks at inflated prices, paid bribes to get government contracts, and then set prices unreasonably high on the railroad routes they controlled.

One of the worst examples of governmental corruption was Boss Tweed in New York City. He gained control of the Democratic Party and absolute control of the city government. He and his ring stole as much as $200 million dollars by overcharging the treasury for goods and services (for example: $138,000 for two days work

| Boss Tweed, with a Thomas Nast caricature of him

by a plasterer). He was brought down by evidence published by the New York *Times* and by the anti-Tweed cartoons of Thomas Nast. (Both refused huge bribes not to publish). New York attorney Samuel Tilden led the prosecution team that finally put Tweed in jail in 1873.

Black Friday. James Fisk and Jay Gould were in the unsavory category of wealthy financial pirates. In 1869 they hatched a scheme to "corner the gold market," which would involve buying up gold and holding it until the price went sky high during a panic. Then they could sell the gold they had at an incredible profit. However, they had to make sure that the U.S. government would not sell its own supply of gold to stabilize the market once the panic began. They paid a large bribe to Grant's brother-in-law to convince the president to hold the government gold.

The pair tried their scheme on "Black Friday," September 24. The price of gold shot up, driving many businessmen to near ruin. However, Grant did not block the sale of government gold and the whole scheme collapsed. A congressional investigation did not implicate Grant, but the scandal did touch his family.

Crédit Mobilier. Another scandal hit the administration in 1872. Crédit Mobilier was a railroad construction company created by officers of the Union Pacific Railway. They used the company to build the transcontinental railroad, charging double the actual construction costs. The owners made sure Washington would not interfere by giving Crédit Mobilier stock to key congressmen and Grant's vice-president. When it was exposed by a newspaper, it reflected badly on the lack of control and honesty in the government. Pressure for reform began to mount.

Alabama Claims. During the Civil War, Britain had allowed ships to be built for the Confederacy in British shipyards. They were fitted with guns in other countries and were used to raid Union shipping throughout the war. The most notorious was the *Alabama*. The ship was built in Britain, armed in Portugal, and sailed by a British crew! It never entered a Confederate port, even though it flew a Confederate flag and captured over sixty Union merchant vessels. U.S. officials in Britain had been pressing the British government to pay for damages caused by that and other British/Confederate privateers.

The British government felt the pressure to settle the dispute, for their officials felt the claim was legitimate. Others feared a bad precedent if a revolt broke out in Ireland, and America supplied them with the same type of raiders. So in 1871, Britain and the U.S. signed the Treaty of Washington which submitted the entire dispute to an arbitration panel in Geneva, Switzerland. The arbitrators awarded the U.S. $15.5 million. The award restored good relations between the two nations.

Election of 1872. By 1872 the scandals of "Grantism" had created a large reform movement. Reformers in the Republican party refused to support Grant when it was clear he would run again. Instead, they formed the Liberal Republican Party and nominated Horace Greeley, the famous editor of the New York *Tribune*. Greeley was a bad choice due to his ragged appearance, lack of flexibility, and emotionalism. The Democrats, desperate for office, also supported the rabidly anti-Confederate Greeley.

After a vicious campaign, Grant won the election with a larger margin than in 1868. As with most third-party movements in U.S. history, the Liberal Republicans were absorbed into one of the larger parties once it took over their ideals. In this case, the Republicans sponsored tariff reform, amnesty for Confederate leaders, and a wave toward civil service reform, all of which stole the reformer's thunder.

| Horace Greeley, editor of the New York Tribune and Liberal Republican Presidential Candidate

Panic of 1873. Grant's second term had a hard shock when the nation went into a financial panic in 1873. The country had again overextended on credit. When purchases no longer kept up with what businesses needed to pay their debts, the economy crashed. It began with the bankruptcy of a large New York banking firm and quickly spread as thousands of other companies folded. It was the nation's longest depression to date, lasting six years.

The government of that day did not even consider using tax dollars to fix the economy. That was well understood to be the job of private businesses <u>only</u>. However, there was a vigorous debate over a correct monetary policy that would aid the economy. "Hard money" people wanted all money to be gold, silver, or paper notes backed by a certain amount of gold. "Soft" or "cheap money" advocates wanted paper money that circulated without a set value. The latter causes inflation and makes it easier for debtors to pay off their debts. It is known today that a hard money policy decreases the money supply and when begun during a depression it tends to make the depression worse.

Grant was a hard money man. He supported the Resumption Act of 1875 that promised to redeem all Civil War-issued paper money for its face value in gold. That decision worsened the depression and gave the Democrats control of the House of Representatives after the 1874 elections. It led to the creation of another third party called the Greenbacks who elected several members of Congress in 1878.

Further Scandals. Yet another scandal, the Whiskey Ring, surfaced in 1875. It was a system of payoffs designed to cheat the government out of money from the whiskey excise tax. Treasury agents took bribes to ignore untaxed whiskey. It was uncovered by a new secretary of the treasury and implicated several of President Grant's friends, including his personal secretary. Grant allowed the investigation at first, but began to interfere with it as it touched his friends. Eventually, the secretary was tried and Grant obtained his acquittal by sending the court a letter saying the president believed he was innocent.

William Belknap, Grant's secretary of war, was impeached in 1876 for taking bribes from men who received contracts to supply goods to the Native Americans. The supplier made a handsome profit by giving the Native Americans inferior goods while charging for quality ones. Belknap resigned, managing to avoid a conviction. The string of scandals severely damaged Grant's reputation.

Name these items, events, or people.

3.40 _____ policy that called for all money to be gold, silver, or paper notes backed by a certain amount of gold

3.41 _____ Democratic candidate in 1868

3.42 _____ Democrat who ran New York City, stealing millions

3.43 _____ company that constructed track for the Union Pacific, charging way over the costs and giving stock to congressmen

3.44 _____ law that promised to redeem all Civil War paper money for gold

3.45 _____ scheme to cheat the government out of excise tax income

3.46 _____ third party created by Grant's hard money policy

3.47 _____ treaty that submitted the *Alabama* dispute to arbitration

3.48 _____ plan to end rewarding political supporters with government jobs

3.49 _____ name given the day Fisk and Gould tried to corner the gold market

3.50 _____ third party that sought reform in 1872

3.51 _____ secretary of war, resigned over bribery scandal

3.52 _____ amount of money awarded to the U.S. for *Alabama* claims

3.53 _____ cartoonist who helped bring down Boss Tweed

Answer true or false.

3.54 _____ Ulysses S. Grant was a great president.

3.55 _____ "Waving the bloody shirt" was reminding the electorate of the war.

3.56 _____ Grant was dishonest.

3.57 _____ The Democratic Party absorbed the Liberal Republicans by taking their ideas.

3.58 _____ During his administration, Grant's brother-in-law, personal secretary, and secretary of war were implicated in bribery scandals.

3.59 _____ "Vote as you shot" was a Democratic slogan.

3.60 _____ Corruption was a major problem in government and business after the Civil War.

End of Reconstruction

Election of 1876. Grant, encouraged by his political leeches, seriously considered running for a third term. By large majority, the House of Representatives published a resolution opposing third terms as protection against dictators. Grant took the point, and the Republicans looked for another man.

The former president proved as inept in business after the war as he had been before it. He invested his savings in a banking company called Grant & Ward. Ward was dishonest, and Grant lost everything in 1884 when the company failed. He started writing articles about the Civil War in order to support his family, but shortly after that he developed throat cancer (he was a heavy cigar smoker). He wrote his memoirs as the disease slowly took his life. He died soon after it was completed, and the success of the book gave his family a very comfortable income. The Civil War was the one pure success of Ulysses S. Grant.

The Republicans almost nominated Maine congressman James Blaine, but evidence of a bribery scandal ended his chances. America was tired of corruption and wanted an honest candidate. The Republicans finally chose Rutherford B. Hayes, governor of Ohio and a Union war veteran. He had been an honest, competent governor and supported civil service reform. The Democrats chose Samuel Tilden, governor of New York and one of key men in smashing the Tweed Ring, to oppose Hayes. The Republicans again waved the bloody shirt while the Democrats condemned the years of scandal-ridden Republican rule.

Tilden won the popular vote by a small margin and clearly had 184 out of the 185 electoral votes needed to win the election. Hayes had 165 electoral votes. The remaining electoral votes were in dispute. The Republican and Democratic parties submitted different totals for four states: Oregon, Louisiana, Florida, and South Carolina. Hayes needed twenty of these

to win, and the Republicans claimed that he had them. (There were grounds for the dispute. For example, in South Carolina there were more votes than registered voters, and the Ku Klux Klan was busy all over the South stopping Republican votes.)

The Republican Senate and the Democratic House fought over which had authority to settle the dispute. In the end, they set up a joint committee with seven Senate Republicans, seven House Democrats, and one independent, a member of the Supreme Court, to decide the issue. At the last minute, the only independent on the Court resigned, leaving only Republicans, which gave that party an 8 to 7 majority on the election committee. Not surprisingly, the committee gave all of the disputed votes to Hayes by an 8 to 7 vote. Democrats threatened to **filibuster** the acceptance of the results, and some were talking about taking up arms. By now it was February, and the new president was supposed to take office on March 4th.

Compromise of 1877. Eventually, the two sides worked out a compromise. The Democrats agreed to accept the election of Hayes in exchange for the end of Reconstruction. Hayes also promised, but did not deliver, subsidies for a transcontinental railroad in the South. As a result of the Compromise of 1877, Hayes was named the president-elect just three days before inauguration. The deal kept the peace, but gave Southern white people complete control of their states without further fear of federal intervention.

Rutherford B. Hayes (1822-1893). Rutherford B. Hayes entered the White House with much of the nation doubting he had won the election. Hayes had been born **posthumously** to a prosperous store owner in Ohio. His uncle became his guardian and saw that he had a good private school education. He graduated from Harvard in 1842 and took up the practice of law in Ohio. He served as an officer in the

Civil War, reaching the temporary rank of major general. He was elected to the U.S. House while still in combat. (He refused to leave his post to campaign, but won anyway.) He also served three terms as governor of Ohio before he was chosen as president. His was the most questionable election in U.S. history.

Hayes removed the last Union troops from occupation duty shorty after taking office in 1877. This was the official end of Reconstruction. Hayes pushed for civil service reform, but the spoils-minded Congress refused to pass it. Hayes himself appointed men based on ability, not party loyalty, which earned the wrath of the Republicans. Hayes supported hard money policies that did not help the depression, but did build confidence in the security of the American monetary system.

Hayes' wife, Lucy Webb Hayes, had a college degree. She was the first among the nation's First Ladies to have one. She was active in many social causes, including abolition and temperance. She earned the nickname "Lemonade Lucy" because she banned alcoholic beverages from the White House. She and her husband introduced the custom of an annual Easter egg roll for children on the White House lawn.

| Rutherford B. Hayes

Conclusion. The Civil War settled two issues: slavery and secession. Other positive results were more elusive. Black people were free, guaranteed citizenship and the right to vote by constitutional amendments, but those rights were flagrantly violated. However, those amendments were on the books and would be effectively resurrected years later. The South remained a hostile place for black people, Republicans, and Northerners for many years. After winning the war, the North lacked the will or political skill to reintegrate the nation on friendly terms. Given the nature of a civil war, perhaps that was impossible.

The Union was actually lenient to the Confederacy. No Confederate leaders were ever tried for treason. Jefferson Davis was kept in custody for two years and then released. Robert E. Lee was allowed to return home unmolested and became the president of Washington College, later named Washington and Lee. The South was fully represented in Congress by 1870, and the original privileged class was back in power by 1877. Considering that they led an armed rebellion against the government, this was an amazing show of tolerance. Awful as it was, the Civil War barely interrupted the American tradition of growth, expansion, and democracy.

Answer these questions.

3.61 What was the heart of the controversy in the 1876 election?

_____

_____

3.62 How did Hayes fight the spoils system?

_____

_____

3.63 What two issues did the Civil War settle?

_____

3.64 What were the terms of the Compromise of 1877?

_____

_____

_____

3.65 What was the official end of Reconstruction?

_____

3.66 Why was Hayes awarded all the disputed votes in the election of 1876?

_____

_____

3.67 What were some of the unusual things about First Lady Lucy Hayes?

_____

_____

3.68 Who was the Democratic candidate in 1876, and what were his qualifications?

_____

_____

3.69 How many Confederate leaders were tried for treason?

_____

3.70 What were Hayes' qualifications for president?

_____

_____

Before you take this last Self Test, you may want to do one or more of these self checks.

1. _____ Read the objectives. See if you can do them.
2. _____ Restudy the material related to any objectives that you cannot do.
3. _____ Use the **SQ3R** study procedure to review the material:
   a. **S**can the sections.
   b. **Q**uestion yourself.
   c. **R**ead to answer your questions.
   d. **R**ecite the answers to yourself.
   e. **R**eview areas you did not understand.
4. _____ Review all vocabulary, activities, and Self Tests, writing a correct answer for every wrong answer.

SELF TEST 3

Name the event, item, person, or battle (each answer, 4 points).

3.01 _____ first U.S. president in history to be impeached

3.02 _____ "Seward's Folly"

3.03 _____ Amendment that ended slavery

3.04 _____ Democratic hoodlum who ran New York City after the Civil War

3.05 _____ Grant-era scandal; railroad construction scam that gave stock to several government representatives

3.06 _____ Amendment that gave black Americans the right to vote

3.07 _____ Reconstruction under Congressional control

3.08 _____ post-Civil War laws to subjugate black people in the South

3.09 _____ Presidential document that ended slavery in the South

3.010 _____ Amendment that made black Americans citizens

3.011 _____ Hayes was awarded the election in exchange for removing the last troops from the South

3.012 _____ first state to secede from the Union

3.013 _____ Union victory that placed the whole Mississippi under their control

3.014 _____ Northern men who came to power in the South during Reconstruction

3.015 _____ began the Civil War

Choose the person who best fits the description (each answer, 2 points).

Abraham Lincoln   Ulysses S. Grant   Robert E. Lee

Rutherford B. Hayes   Thaddeus Stevens   Stonewall Jackson

Stephen Douglas   Dred Scott   Jefferson Davis

John Brown

3.016 _____ little education; Illinois attorney; flexible; good organizer

3.017 _____ an enslaved man who asked the Supreme Court to set him free after living in the North

3.018 _____ had trouble maintaining authority over the independent-minded Confederacy; imprisoned for two years after the war

3.019 _____ brilliant general; followed his state not his nation; college president

3.020 _____ Radical Republican leader

3.021 _____ opposed Lecompton Constitution; Northern Democratic candidate for president (1860); supported popular sovereignty

3.022 _____ violent; possibly insane; became a popular abolitionist martyr

3.023 _____ good general; honest; corrupt administration; Whiskey Ring

3.024 _____ Southern; Christian general; killed by his own men

3.025 _____ Union officer; governor of Ohio; opposed the spoils system; most controversial presidential election in history

Answer true or false (each answer, 1 point).

3.026 _____ Lincoln supported harsh measures against the South after the war.

3.027 _____ Andrew Johnson was the only Southern senator who did not secede with his state.

3.028 _____ Alaska was purchased from Russia for $7.2 million by Secretary of State William Seward.

3.029 _____ The Ku Klux Klan was very ineffective after the Civil War.

3.030 _____ Scalawags were army deserters during the Civil War.

3.031 _____ Republicans after the war often campaigned by "waving the bloody shirt."

3.032 _____ George McClellan was an excellent organizer, but so over-cautious that he proved to be a poor general.

3.033 _____ Grant was not thrown out of the army after Shiloh because Lincoln would not fire a general who was willing to fight.

3.034 _____ Abolitionist Senator Charles Sumner was beaten in the Senate for an anti-Southern speech.

3.035 _____ The Kansas-Nebraska Act brought the nation closer to war.

3.036 _____ The battle of the *Merrimac* and the *Monitor* was the first in history between ironclad vessels.

3.037 _____ Fredericksburg, Chickamauga, and New Orleans were all taken by the Union after a long siege.

3.038 _____ Copperheads were Northern Democrats who opposed the war.

3.039 _____ The re-election of Lincoln in 1864 ended the last Confederate hope of a negotiated peace that would leave them independent.

3.040 _____ The Civil War effectively ended at Appomattox Court House when Lee's army surrendered.

3.041 _____ The Confederate government was formed before Lincoln was inaugurated.

3.042 _____ The *Alabama* was a British-built ship with a British crew that sailed under a Confederate flag and captured Union ships.

3.043 _____ Fisk and Gould tried to corner the oil market on black Thursday.

3.044 _____ Corruption was a major problem in government and industry after the Civil War.

3.045 _____ The assassination of Lincoln made matters worse for the South.

80 / 100   SCORE _____   TEACHER _____ _____
                                              initials   date

Before taking the LIFEPAC Test, you may want to do one or more of these self checks.

1. _____ Read the objectives. See if you can do them.

2. _____ Restudy the material related to any objectives that you cannot do.

3. _____ Use the **SQ3R** study procedure to review the material.

4. _____ Review activities, Self Tests, and LIFEPAC vocabulary words.

5. _____ Restudy areas of weakness indicated by the last Self Test.

HISTORY & GEOGRAPHY 806

LIFEPAC TEST

NAME _____

DATE _____

SCORE _____

HISTORY & GEOGRAPHY 806: LIFEPAC TEST

Choose the <u>best</u> answer (each answer, 4 points).

1. The North won the Civil War because _____ .
   a. it had better generals
   b. it had more resources
   c. the South could not break the blockade

2. The most important failure of Reconstruction was _____ .
   a. share cropping
   b. not adequately protecting the rights of freedmen
   c. Southern corruption

3. The greatest cause of the high numbers of dead in the Civil War was _____ .
   a. out of date military tactics
   b. accurate artillery fire
   c. lack of medical knowledge

4. The primary reason for the Civil War was conflict over _____ .
   a. slavery
   b. states' rights
   c. Lincoln's election

5. The Republican Party _____ in 1860.
   a. was abolitionist
   b. opposed states' rights
   c. opposed the extension of slavery

Name the person, event, battle, or item (each answer, 3 points).

6. _____ where the Civil War effectively ended

7. _____ turning point of the Civil War

8. _____ document issued by Lincoln that declared slavery ended in the Confederacy

9. _____ the most brilliant general of the Civil War

10. _____ man who assassinated Lincoln

11. _____ Amendment that ended slavery

12. _____ land called "Seward's Folly"

13. _____ "Four score and seven years ago, our fathers brought forth upon this continent … " (name the speech)

14. _____ one of our worst presidents, had a scandal ridden administration, Union general

15. _____ Union general, devastated Georgia on march to the sea

16. _____ laws passed by Southern states after the Civil War that ensured black people would still be subjugated

17. _____ nickname for Kansas as popular sovereignty was practiced there

18. _____ Supreme Court decision, protected slavery in all states

19. _____ Amendment that made freedmen citizens

20. _____ last attempt at compromise before the Civil War

Answer these questions (each answer, 3 points).

21. What was different about Grant as the Union commander in Virginia?

    _____

22. What was the outcome of Andrew Johnson's impeachment trial?

    _____

    _____

23. Why was the Northern army better supplied that the Southern one?

    _____

    _____

24. Why was the battle of Antietam specifically important to Lincoln?

    _____

    _____

25. What did the South do that caused Congress and the North to challenge Johnson's Reconstruction plans?

    _____

    _____

Match these items (each answer, 2 points).

26. _____ anti-war Northern Democrats

27. _____ scam to cheat the government out of excise tax income

28. _____ prison camp

29. _____ pro-slavery legal document that mocked popular sovereignty in Kansas

30. _____ gave the North control of the Mississippi

31. _____ rude awakening for the Union which had hoped for an easy war

32. _____ used violence to regain white control of the South

33. _____ attempt by John Brown to start a slave uprising

34. _____ made Lincoln a name in national politics

35. _____ early welfare agency, set up schools for former slaves

a. Lecompton Constitution
b. Lincoln-Douglas Debates
c. Harpers Ferry Raid
d. Vicksburg
e. Copperheads
f. Freedmen's Bureau
g. Ku Klux Klan
h. Whiskey Ring
i. First Bull Run
j. Andersonville